WORK WONDERS

WORK WONDERS

Feed your dog
raw meaty bones

TOM LONSDALE

RIVETCO P/L

First published in 2005 by:
Rivetco P/L
PO Box 6096
Windsor Delivery Centre
NSW 2756
Australia

Telephone: +61 2 4574 0537
E-mail: rivetco@rawmeatybones.com
Web: www.rawmeatybones.com

National Library of Australia Cataloguing-in-Publication entry:

Lonsdale, Tom, 1949-
Work wonders: feed your dog raw meaty bones.

Bibliography.
Includes index.
ISBN 0 9757174 0 5.

1. Dogs - Food. 2. Dogs - Nutrition. 3. Dogs - Health. 4. Raw foods.

636. 7085

This book has been written and published in good faith. However, when dealing with biological systems, for instance the health of animals, problems can occur. The publisher is therefore unable to guarantee that, in every circumstance, the information presented here will be of benefit and neither does the information constitute professional advice upon which you should rely.

If you find errors of fact or interpretation contained within these pages please contact the publisher.

Cover design and typesetting: Lankshear Design.
Cover and internal illustrations: Bonny Bullock.

Contents

Tom Lonsdale VETERINARY SURGEON

PO Box 6096
Windsor Delivery Centre
NSW 2756
Australia

E-mail: tom@rawmeatybones.com
Web: www.rawmeatybones.com

September 2005

Dear Reader,

Sometimes a lucky coincidence or chance encounter helps throw new light on an old situation. That's what happened to me. Finally, after five years at veterinary school and fifteen years as a qualified vet, I saw that processed foods do immense harm and natural foods work wonders for the health of dogs and other carnivores.

At first I was aghast, but then was uplifted. Here was the answer to so many of the problems facing my patients.

If you own an adult dog that you feed on canned or packaged food, now is the time to make a change. If you have a young puppy then starting him or her on a more natural diet should work wonders.

Here's wishing you and your canine companions the best of good health,

Tom Lonsdale

Promote Health

1

Getting started

Many of my canine patients took on a new lease of life, became like puppies again, when I changed their diet to raw meaty bones and a few table scraps. Puppies started on a more natural diet grew healthy and strong and seldom needed veterinary care. Perhaps I should not have been surprised; for Nature works wonders in numerous ways and a diet of raw meaty bones plus a few scraps approximates to the natural diet of dogs in the wild. How and why natural food works wonders are questions needing answers. For now, though, we can tap into the benefits, we can feed our dogs raw meaty bones.

This back-to-basics approach puts us in touch with the inner needs of our dogs—and it's easy.

Throughout the book I refer to Nature's teachings so that if you are stuck for an answer you can refer to Nature too. As you gain in confidence, you may want to share your discoveries. 'Think of Nature' tell your friends and neighbors when you want them to savor the simplicity and joy of feeding dogs the natural way.

Once you make a start many things will help reinforce your commitment:

- The looks of contentment on furry faces.
- The satisfying crunch of teeth shearing bone.
- Trim, taught, terrific pets free from debilitating diseases.

- Vet bills that decline or disappear.
- Natural feeding provides a tonic for humans too.

You will appreciate that Nature does not affix labels to things or distinguish between food and medicine. Natural food cures and prevents a range of diseases—it's the ideal medicine.

- You will step off the commercial merry-go-round of the junk pet-food industry and the veterinary profession and be part of a movement for a better world, free of ill health and suffering.
- You will gain in confidence as a result of your increased understanding and closer contact with Nature.

It's not new

It's not new, it's just that we forgot and then let commercial interests take control. Hippocrates, the famous Greek physician in the 5th century BC, said:

Leave your drugs in the chemist's pot if you can heal your patients with food.[1]

Animals in the wild instinctively know what's good for them. If they wish to stay well they need to be well fed. Hence a lion's willingness to face off against a full-grown buffalo bull. Imagine if your dinner came charging at you, 2000 pounds of muscle and bone, intent on flattening you. For the big cats the importance of a correct diet requires that they take risks every time they feel hungry.

Wolves, the predecessors of our domestic dogs, are similarly driven to make huge efforts to stay well fed and healthy. Running through deep snow takes energy and, once they close in for the kill, wolves risk injury from sharp hooves and horns.

In Australia dingoes, dogs that escaped domestication, lead

a tough life in the mountains and arid range lands. No fireside rug in the winter or airconditioned comfort in the summer for them. Instead they depend on catching the right food for survival and an opportunity to breed. In areas where easy-to-catch sheep and goats are plentiful packs of dingoes still prefer to hunt kangaroos and wallabies.[2] Yes; it comes down to the quality of the meat and bone. The dingoes' natural instincts lead them to expend more effort to obtain the best—good quality food and medicine comes at a price.

If you watch the TV Discovery Channel you'll see carnivores doing what Nature intended—catching and consuming whole carcasses of other animals. If our pet dogs had the chance, that's what they would be doing too.

Note: Catching *carcasses*, not catching meat. Our name for predatory animals is *carnivore*, meaning meat eater. But that's only part of the truth. If we feed lions, wolves or dogs on meat and meat alone then problems arise. It's essential that predators have lots of bone in the diet so that their own bones grow strong. If we described our predatory animals as *carcassivores* I believe we would already be halfway to understanding their dietary needs and thus preparing to meet those needs—whole carcasses of other animals.

At this point you may be feeling a little nervous. Chances are you and your pets live in a civilized place far removed from the wilderness of Discovery Channel documentaries. Please relax. We need firm foundations. We need to establish what Nature had in mind. Once we've done that we shall have a sound base upon which to build a raw meaty bones and table scraps alternative that provides ease, economy and efficiency for modern pet owners.

Chemical and physical—food and medicine

Let's contemplate for a moment what wild predators obtain when they eat whole carcasses of other animals as opposed to the canned mush or dry kibble out of a packet—the so called food but not medicine of the average domestic pet.

The chemicals, we call them nutrients, in carcasses are ideal for the energy, growth and body-repair needs of carnivores. But more than that, the right quality and quantity of nutrients ensure tiptop functioning of all body systems. And that's what we mean by being in *good health*—body systems, free of stress, functioning well and supporting each other. Hence we can say that the proper diet provides *medicinal* benefits.

Nature's grand design includes the physical form and texture of the food too. Carnivores need nutrients—proteins, fats, minerals, vitamins and trace elements—and those nutrients need to be raw, tough and chewy.

By ripping, tearing and crunching their way through tough, chewy carcasses (or large pieces of raw meaty bones) carnivores also wash, scrub and polish their teeth and gums. We humans maintain dental hygiene by tooth brushing and flossing after we eat. Carnivores brush and floss *as they eat*. Clean teeth and gums are an essential part of what it means to be *healthy*.

Most pets fed processed food have dirty, plaque-laden teeth and sore gums. The bacteria in plaque produce foul gases—that's where the term 'dog breath' comes from. 'Dog breath' is bad enough, but it's the impact of diseased teeth and gums, periodontal disease, on the rest of the body that is the major reason for concern. Research shows that animals with periodontal disease are more likely to suffer from liver, kidney and immune system problems.[3] Affected animals are often caught in a downward spiral of ill health.

Ripping and tearing raw meat from bones takes time and

effort—and hence confers other benefits. Muscles of the jaws, neck and chest gain exercise, digestive juices flow, neurological and immune systems get a boost.[4] The life force of carnivores directs them to devour carcasses. Ripping and tearing their food stimulates the flow of brain chemicals which in turn help tone the hormonal and immune systems—that's the essence of wellbeing.[5]

Digestive enzymes in the stomach and intestines are designed to work on food of the correct chemical and physical composition. In the colon (large bowel), healthy animals have a large population of bacteria necessary for the final digestive stages. When the correct chemical and physical balance is upset then unwelcome bacteria proliferate—with resultant bad smells, diarrhea and worse.[6]

Did you notice the suitable nutrients listed included proteins and fats but carbohydrates didn't get a mention? That's because dogs have no known requirement for carbohydrates in the diet.[7] Carbohydrates come from the starches in grains and the sugars in fruit. Cellulose, another carbohydrate, gives plants their fibrous structure and makes for the bulky fecal deposits of herbivores. The occasional slice of bread or left-over pasta is unlikely to do much harm to your dog. It's the regular feeding of grain based commercial diets—neither chemically nor physically suitable—that do intense harm.

Grain in processed food is poorly digested and leads to soft, bulky dog droppings that foul parks and gardens the world over. Pets fed raw carcasses or a diet based on raw meaty bones produce a fraction of the waste. Odors are minimal and the droppings turn chalky white in the sun.

Healthy skepticism

If Nature got it so right how then did we, as a society, get it so wrong? Various answers could be advanced, but one common denominator seems to be our misplaced trust in so called 'experts'.

During human evolution our ancestors, living in caves and make-shift shelters, provided the ancestors of modern dogs with an excellent diet—whole carcasses when available, otherwise raw meaty bones, offal and leftover scraps. Chances are our ancestors devoted little or no thought to the matter of diets for dogs. They did what came naturally.

For us, our thoughts and actions are conditioned by the words of experts. We discuss feeding, not in terms of how to throw a carcass out of the cave, but in terms of calories, proteins and fats and a host of specialized concepts implanted in our minds by experts.

When it comes to the practical aspects of feeding our pets the pet-food company experts have taken charge. Packaged, cooked, pulverized grains in cans and packets leave the conveyor belt and appear as eye-catching displays on supermarket shelves. Experts in advertising and marketing craft the TV commercials and experts working for government regulatory departments condone the production of unsuitable, unsafe products promoted with a constant stream of misinformation.

Over a number of years, as our pets became sicker with failing hearts, kidneys, immune systems, dog breath and skin disease the veterinary experts assumed control. Seldom if ever blaming the artificial and harmful diets, (many) veterinary experts blame the failing body systems. 'A weak heart', 'a defective immune system', 'failing kidneys' they say. And when the veterinary experts cannot stem the tide of sick bedraggled animals, they call for more research and open more veterinary schools to train more experts.

Yes, our ancestors who domesticated the wolf and then developed the dog breeds we know today did what came naturally at little or no cost and the food they fed worked wonders. We place our trust in experts and pay a high price. Our pets pay with their lives.

How then to break free from the multiple strands of misinformation that bind us to the 'experts'? I suggest we need to develop a healthy skepticism—a willingness to doubt all aspects of our cultural conditioning—let our minds travel back to a time when Nature's teachings were the first and only set of instructions. Also, may I suggest that you learn by doing—like a toddler taking first steps. Make a start, and soon you will be reveling in your newfound accomplishment.

2

Quality, quantity, frequency

Let's take a look at the features of a healthy diet—the quality, quantity and frequency of feeding—necessary to maintain our dogs in top condition and minimize trips to the vet.

But before we begin let's focus on three key aspects. If we get these things right the rest should fall into place.

First, do no harm said the early physicians and so it is when feeding dogs. Stop feeding processed grain-based junk foods and already we are halfway to solving the problems of bad nutrition. Benefits are often immediate and lifelong. Resist the urge to provide a bowl of kibble in case your pet gets hungry— good health matters more.

Second, Nature is tolerant, perhaps too tolerant, and permits a range of feeding options. So when we talk about quality, quantity and frequency of feeding we don't have to be exact. Variations can occur and still provide a satisfactory outcome.

Third, if you are a beginner, you may worry about reading ideas written on paper and then converting those ideas into practical action. This is where a coach/mentor comes in handy. Do you have a friend or relative experienced in feeding raw food? Does your vet support raw feeding? Some of the best sources of help and encouragement can be found on the internet raw feeding discussion lists (see Information Resources page 99).

List moderators and experienced raw-feeders provide guidance for newcomers, leavened with patience and spiced with humor—it's free and it's fun.

Quality
Carcasses

Our pet dogs, modified wolves, deserve the best available—whole carcasses of other animals. That, after all, is what responsible zoo keepers feed their captive wolves and wild dogs.

At feeding time the zoo keeper fills the food cart with chilled carcasses of chickens, rabbits, whole fish and large pieces of raw meaty bones. Carcasses likely have the entrails still intact and the fur, feathers and scales just as Nature intended. Wolves, living in the wild, hunt deer, elk and other large prey. Some zoos can obtain deer, but often, when feeding packs of wolves zoo keepers drag the carcasses of farm animals—cattle, sheep, goats—into the wolf pen.

'Feeding frenzy' describes what happens next and at the end there isn't much left—perhaps some hooves or large leg bones or the contents of the rumen (fore-stomach) and colon of a goat. Wolves and wild dogs, when free to choose, distinguish between what's good and what's not good to eat.

When the prey is small, for instance chickens and rabbits, then the entrails may be eaten together with all contents—mostly part digested grasses, and perhaps a few fruits and seeds. Wolves may eat berries and ripe fallen fruit when in season. However, for free living wolves and wild dogs vegetable matter forms a minor part of the diet.

Completing the picture of what wolves and wild dogs consider to be 'quality' food we should note they eat the feces of their prey and, since their dining table is often bare earth, they ingest soil and debris adhering to the fresh carcass.

So the big question: What are you going to do as head keeper in your zoo without bars? Following Nature's model is easily the best option. Table 1 contains several carcass options suitable for dogs but, as mentioned, Nature is flexible and forgiving. Fortunately, the second best option, raw meaty bones and table scraps provides good health, good value and convenience.

Table 1: Carcasses

Carcasses suitable for small dogs
Rats, mice, rabbits, fish, chickens/hens, quail, day-old chicks

Carcasses suitable for large dogs
Rabbits, chickens/hens, fish, calf, goat, pig, kangaroo, lamb.

Raw meaty bones

A diet of predominantly raw meaty bones and a few leftover table scraps provides a tried, tested and successful method of feeding dogs. Numerous dog owners and increasing numbers of veterinarians attest to the ease, economy and efficiency of such a diet.

Key principles

1. Feed meaty bones *raw*.

2. Feed meaty bones in *large pieces* to ensure maximum cleaning of teeth and gums.

3. Feed meaty bones from a *variety* of animals—for instance chicken, lamb and rabbit—thus ensuring good balance of nutrients.

Please keep these principles in mind, but at the same time practical considerations and availability of supplies may influence your decisions.

Table 2: Raw meaty bones

- Chicken and turkey backs and frames after the meat has been removed for human consumption suitable for all dogs

- Poultry heads, feet, necks and wings suitable for very small dogs only

- Whole fish and fish heads

- Goat, sheep, calf, deer and kangaroo carcasses can be sawn into large pieces of meat and bone

- Other by-products include: pigs' trotters, pigs' heads, sheep heads, brisket, tail bones and rib bones

FOOD AND MEDICINE

... SIMPLE CONCEPT, PROFOUND IMPLICATIONS

Raw meaty chicken and turkey bones

Chicken necks and wings make a good, basic diet for tiny dogs. A cheaper, better option are the backs and frames. Poultry processing plants remove the meat fillets for human consumption and the bones are sold for making soup. The bones still carry plenty of meat, are soft and flat and pose little risk of splintering.

Chicken backs and frames can be fed to large-breed dogs too. But at least three days each week I recommend that you feed larger, raw, meaty bones, for instance ox tail or lamb neck, thus ensuring adequate teeth cleaning.

Turkey necks, wings, backs and frames are suitable for most dogs.

Do not feed chicken necks and wings to larger dogs—they tend to swallow the pieces whole with the possible risk of blockage.

Lamb necks, ox and kangaroo tails

Lamb necks, ox and kangaroo tails are good for all breeds of dogs. Providing the bones are meaty and fed as one large piece they make an excellent meal for the larger breeds. Medium, small and tiny dogs gain plenty of exercise tugging and gnawing the meat and sinews off tail and neck bones. Hard bone will likely be discarded, but only after the dogs gain a good work-out.

Sheep, deer and pig heads

Large dogs can devour sheep, deer and pig heads. Smaller dogs, indeed all dogs, benefit if skulls are sawn down the middle. Ask your butcher, he will most likely oblige. (Some countries restrict the sale of animal heads and spinal tissue. See Information Resources page 99.)

Sides of lamb, slabs of beef

If you have several dogs it may be possible to feed them communally on sides of lamb, slabs of beef or similar. In Britain foxhounds are customarily fed as a pack. Puppies of all breeds start out life sharing their meals with litter mates. Please exercise care if you anticipate any uncontrolled aggression.

For individual dogs, feeding several days' supply of food as one large piece, say a shoulder of lamb, works well. Each day, after your dog has eaten his share return the meat and bone to the refrigerator. Sharp canine teeth raking and scything through slabs of meat gain maximum cleaning. Eventually, after a few days, when only the heaviest bones remain, the premolar and molar teeth get a thorough work-out too.

Pork neck and ox brisket bones

Dogs gain lots of pleasure gnawing on relatively soft, edible pork neck and ox brisket bones. Trouble is the proportion of meat relative to the amount of bone makes for firm feces, even constipation. Bones with little or no meat should not form a major part of a dog's diet.

Offal

Offal refers to any of the internal organs: intestines, tripe (the wall of the rumen of cattle, sheep and other ruminants) liver, pancreas, spleen, kidneys, heart and lungs.

All items provide nutrition of good quality, when fed raw and in big pieces, as consumed by wild carnivores ripping into a carcass.

Feed liver as a whole meal once every two weeks. But take care. Animals develop a taste for liver and if fed in excess, on a regular basis, it can create vitamin A excess. (Dried liver training treats are safe for use at any time.)

Pancreas contains a rich supply of digestive enzymes and is especially good for dogs suffering pancreatic insufficiency.

Table 3: Offal

Offal suitable for dogs of all sizes
Liver, lungs, trachea, hearts, omasums (stomach of ruminants), tripe, tongues, pancreas, spleen

Table scraps

Pigs, bears and humans eat a range of plant and animal foods and are classified as omnivores. Sometimes carnivores eat omnivores, including the food in the omnivore's intestines. For this reason feel free to feed your dog leftover table scraps, omnivore food, straight from the plate.

There are a few exceptions mentioned in Chapter 5 page 58, but in general what's good for you is OK and may be beneficial for your pet. Vegetables may need to be puréed or cooked to make them palatable. This applies to the outer leaves of cabbage and other vegetable peelings. Let common sense be your guide. What is inedible for you is most likely inedible for your dog— so don't feed melon rind, outer leaves of artichokes and orange peel. Occasional feeding of a few spoonfuls of boiled rice, leftover ice-cream or a slice of sponge cake should be OK, but starchy, sugary foods should not be fed in large quantity.

Cooked bones should *not* be fed to your dog.

Supplements

Sick and elderly dogs may benefit from some dietary items added as supplements. Healthy dogs fed a healthy diet do not need supplements. (See Chapter 5 page 61) Your veterinarian can advise. Ripe raw fruit, not strictly a supplement, is enjoyed by many dogs. Anti-oxidants and micronutrients in the fruit may be of value, even for carnivores, and appear to do no harm.

Cat feces, soil and vegetation

Have you noticed how dogs search out bird droppings in the park and carefully pick out the deposits from the kitty-litter tray? Unless you like to kiss your dog, don't worry about this natural canine behavior. Fecal material contains enzymes, vitamins and is teeming with bacteria—in a sense teeming with tiny live prey. For dogs forced to eat a diet of factory-made food, the items they scavenge may be the most nutritious.

Dogs may lick the earth, containing bacteria and minerals, and chew on grass and other vegetation. These natural canine activities likely provide benefit and probably do no harm.

Some dogs search out wide blades of grass which, when consumed, stimulate vomiting. It's uncertain why dogs do this; although dogs with periodontal disease (tooth and gum disease) often indulge the habit. We can speculate that stomach acids or perhaps plant chemicals, for instance chlorophyll, may have a medicinal effect on diseased gums.

Quantity
Proportions of raw meaty bones, offal and scraps

Beginners ask how much to feed. Experienced raw feeders don't think about it—their dogs trained them well.

If you feed whole carcasses, skin and guts intact, then you will be close to Nature's ideal. However, some carcasses are lean and others fat. The proportion of intestines in a fish is small by comparison with a chicken and smaller still when compared with a rabbit. Rabbit bones make up about 8% of their body weight and elephant bones make up 16.5% of theirs.[1,2]

When feeding raw meaty bones as the basis of a diet we need to make an informed assessment of the proportion of meaty bones to feed. Meat, bone and skin make up about 78% of the weight of a deer carcass.[3] As a reasonable rule of thumb for feeding your dog I suggest you supply 70% of the diet as raw, *meaty*, bones. Feed the daily ration in large pieces and, within reason, it doesn't seem to matter what else makes up the balance of the diet.

Some people can obtain green tripe, heart, lung, ox cheek, tongue, etc and feed these items to make up the other 22% of the 'deer prey-model'. I applaud those who do their best to mimic Nature. Others who have access to a ready supply of sheep and cattle omasums (fore-stomach) feed those in large quantity with only the occasional meaty bone. For adult dogs this is a cheap and satisfactory way of feeding.

Most people can obtain ox, lamb or pig's liver. Liver contains high quality proteins, fat, enzymes and vitamins. A large meal of liver every two weeks provides a useful addition to a raw meaty bones and table scraps diet.

If it is not possible to access offal, feeding raw meaty bones, even up to 100% of the diet, promotes health with few if any problems.*** When I ran a busy veterinary practice, many of my clients fed almost exclusively chicken backs and frames—whether to adult dogs or litters of puppies—and their animals showed excellent health.

Quantities of table scraps fed vary enormously. Some people feed few if any table scraps; others purée fresh vegetables and serve regular amounts of ripe fruit. But the governing factor ensuring the health of dogs appears to be the basis of the diet—raw meaty bones.

(*** After years of neglect much research needs to be done. Please see www.rawmeatybones.com for updates and reports on the latest research.)

Daily rations

Fresh water should always be available.

No doubt there are nutritionists in laboratories and universities who can tell you the daily food requirements for people of all ages and sizes. Mothers I know don't have that information, but their children are well fed and contented. The same applies for our pet dogs. If your dog carries excess weight you need to feed less and if he or she is on the thin side you may need to feed more. (Some breeds, for instance salukis and whippets, often look thin, and sick dogs often lose weight—your vet can advise.)

Viewed from above does your dog have a satisfactory indent at the waistline or is there a bulge? In short-coated breeds look for a faint outline of the ribs. No outline means too fat. Like a washboard means your pet needs extra food. If your pet has a thicker coat, try running your fingers over its ribs. Do the ribs ripple under your fingers? Check your own ribs for comparison. What's the verdict? – Too thin, too fat or just right?

Other factors help in determining how much to feed.

Is your pet:
- big or small?
- lively?
- eager for food?

Does your pet:
- quickly consume food or leave some uneaten?
- bury bones in the backyard? (a sign of overfeeding)

Like us, our pets' appetites vary between individuals and individual appetites vary from day to day. And of course hard working dogs, pregnant and nursing mothers need more food than the average.

As a guide, the raw meaty bones *average* needs of small dogs tends to be about 3% of their own body weight daily or 21% of body weight spread over a week. Supplementary table scraps may contribute extra.

So, in round terms a 10 pound dog consumes about 2 pounds of food each week. Or, if you measure in kilograms, then a 5 kg dog likely needs about 1 kg of raw meaty bones over the course of a week.

Fortunately most big dogs need less food, even as low as 1% of their body weight daily or 7% weekly.

Frequency
Adult dogs

In the wild, carnivores feed at random intervals. In domestic settings a regular routine tends to work best.

For adult dogs I recommend feeding once daily. Feeding on the bare earth outside is best. But in severe weather, and for other reasons, the kitchen/laundry/shower recess may be a better option. Some people prefer to confine their dogs to crates to ensure no stealing or fighting. Forget about bowls. Carcasses or raw meaty bones will soon be dragged to a comfortable spot—another reason why bedrooms have doors.

Growing puppies

Puppies fed raw food from an early age seldom overeat. From three weeks of age they can be provided with a constant supply of raw food and water thus permitting the puppies to choose when to eat, when to drink, when to rest and when to play.

If your puppy tends to become too fat or for management reasons you don't want raw meat lying around, then feed three meals per day up to four months of age. From four months of age meals can be provided two times per day. Between six and twelve months of age, depending on size and maturity of your puppy, meals can be reduced to once daily.

Growing puppies of the large breeds, depending on their genetic makeup, may have a tendency to develop bone and joint problems. Large breed puppies need plenty of *rest, no forced exercise* and should be kept *slim*. From one year of age exercise can be increased, but until then keep exercise restrictions in force. This is the best way to limit problems with growing bones and joints.

Time

In general I favor evening time for feeding pets. In the cool of the evening flies and ants tend not to be troublesome. It's also a time when family members can supervise the feast.

Dogs tend to sleep well after a good feed. If, however, your pets get to know the set routine and drool and pester you; then perhaps consider making meal times random.

Temperature

In temperate and warm climates food can be fed direct from the refrigerator or freezer—it soon thaws or can be eaten frozen, like ice-cream.

Fasting

Carnivores tend to regulate their own food intake. Even if raw carcasses or raw meaty bones are constantly available many dogs do not overeat. In the wild fasting between hunts is normal and research evidence suggests that fasting confers health benefits.[4]

Well fed, healthy dogs can be fasted one or two days each week. This is especially advantageous if you have miscalculated and run out of food. Simply feed a bigger quantity the next day.

Except under veterinary supervision, elderly and sick dogs and young puppies should not be fasted.

3

Raw resources

Animals shriek, grunt and growl, onlookers ooh and aah when it's feeding time at the zoo. It's the main event of the day. Responsible zoo managers ensure they do not disappoint the animals or the visitors—they plan ahead. With safety the first principle, they design and build facilities to meet or exceed requirements. Safe viewing areas need to be provided for visitors and safe working conditions for the animal keepers.

Zoos must ensure dependable year-round supplies of appropriate food items at affordable prices. Feeding animals cannot be left to chance.

In your zoo without bars, home to a variable number of dogs and perhaps other carnivores, a little advance planning will help ensure the smooth, efficient feeding of your hungry companions.

Home facilities
Raw meaty bones passed for human consumption

If your dogs are small or few in number then feeding raw meaty bones fit for human consumption is an economical, efficient way to proceed. Your existing refrigerator/freezer probably has sufficient capacity to store a few extra pounds/kilos of food. Try estimating the weekly consumption of your dog. As a guide allow 20% of an animal's body weight in food per week.

A ten pound dog requires about two pounds of food (a 5 kg dog requires 1 kg). If your dog weighs 40 pounds then it will need around eight pounds of food per week (a 20 kg dog will need around 4kg). Do you have sufficient storage space?

It's a good idea to divide the supplies into daily meals. Plastic bags from the grocery store can be reused. Alternatively, you might like to acquire plastic containers which can be stacked in the freezer and then washed after use.

Since the food you are using is 'human-grade' then normal household hygiene provisions should suffice. Make sure seepage from raw meat does not contaminate other foods. Bench tops, food preparation surfaces and utensils should be thoroughly cleaned. Hot water and household detergents work well. Automatic dishwashers take the hard work out of cleaning containers and knives. After handling raw food, wash hands well and ensure small children don't explore with their fingers.

Carcasses, road kill and bulk supplies

The equations change if you buy in bulk, feed whole carcasses (rats, mice, rabbits etc), green tripe, road kill or food not passed for human consumption. Nutritional benefits and ongoing cost savings make this a worthwhile venture. But some initial planning and investment may be necessary.

First, it's a good idea to set aside an area of your laundry, garage or outbuilding for housing refrigerators and freezers. Separate cleaning areas equipped with drainage, hot and cold water are advisable too.

Refrigerators and cool rooms are OK for keeping meat for up to two weeks. But generally, it's best to invest in a separate freezer or maybe a couple of extra freezers.

Upright freezers allow easier access to the stored food and rotation of stock. When feeding lots of animals in the veterinary hospital I found that three tub-freezers facilitated good stock rotation. When two freezers were cleared of stock we made a trip to the poultry plant and returned with large garbage bins full of fresh chicken backs and frames. The chicken was transferred to ice-cream buckets and stacked in the freezers. Cylindrical buckets permit air circulation and rapid freezing of the contents.

Each evening we transferred one or two buckets of frozen chicken to a refrigerator. We needed to separate the large blocks of chicken so, for us, thawing the food was essential. Sometimes we fed whole fish, lamb necks and kangaroo tails. These items were packed individually and fed frozen.

If you pack individual daily rations in your freezer, then thawing the food is unnecessary. Dogs will eat their food frozen.

If you prefer to feed thawed food then best to thaw food overnight in the refrigerator or place the frozen item in a bowl of cold water. Microwave thawing creates 'warm' spots through the meat and is not recommended.

Potential problems with freezing

Small prey animals, for instance day-old chicks, rats and rabbits, can be snap-frozen complete with entrails feathers and fur. However, if freshly killed animals are placed in the freezer ensure plenty of air space to permit rapid freezing.

Freshly killed chickens that are snap-frozen with entrails intact should be safe to feed to pets. But beware, busy poultry plants process thousands of carcasses an hour. Rejected carcasses may be tossed in a bin, and by the end of the day the warm carcasses are already decomposing. Do not freeze decomposing chicken carcasses.

If you are fortunate to have access to whole carcasses of larger animals—deer, sheep, goats, etc—then you will need to butcher and store the meat.

Large carcasses should *not* be frozen with the entrails still intact. Whilst it's possible the entrails will freeze before decomposition takes place, the main problem arises when the carcass thaws. A long, slow thaw permits further decomposition and the potential for the growth of bacterial toxins.

Keep in mind large pieces of meat and bone provide the best canine jaw exercise and teeth cleaning. So whether you do your own butchering or have a professional do it for you, ensure that the pieces are kept large.

You will most likely want to store the meaty bones in plastic bags which, in turn, can be placed in cardboard boxes or on plastic trays. Allow space for air circulation and keep the plastic bags dry. Removal of packages from the freezer should be a simple matter. You don't need to be head first, crowbar in hand, prizing packages from a frozen lake at the bottom of your freezer—your time is too valuable and the plastic lining of your freezer too fragile.

Table scraps and vegetable peel

Table scraps can be fed straight from the plate. Vegetable peelings can be made more appetizing and more digestible by lightly cooking or processing in the kitchen mixer.

Ripe fruit can be fed whole—although take care not to feed pits/stones from peaches, apricots, etc.

Except in rare instances—feeding toothless pets or those with unusual digestive diseases—you will not need a meat and bone grinder. If you need ground meat and bone, then ask your butcher to put some chicken necks through his grinder.

Feeding areas

Where is the best place to feed your pets? With the safety of pets and people in mind, where ever it's most convenient for you.

Some people are deterred from feeding natural food for fear of damaging their deep-pile carpets. This need not be so. Even the smallest living accommodation has a shower recess or tiled laundry where dogs can consume raw food. Confining your dog in a crate at meal times creates a happy association between crate and food. It also permits you to observe the feeding process and ensure that choking, whilst a negligible risk, does not occur.

Dogs can be trained to eat on spread newspaper. But in general carnivores like to drag their food to a secluded spot to enjoy the meal, undisturbed. Accordingly, I consider that dogs are best fed outside—no food bowls necessary. Just throw the carcasses/raw meaty bones on the ground and your pet's natural instincts will take care of the rest. At your discretion, and depending on the weather and fly population, part-eaten bones can be left for further gnawing over ensuing days.

Potential drawbacks to feeding outside are that your pet

may dig holes in the flowerbeds to bury the bones. Your neighbors, at first, may not be used to seeing animal parts scattered across your lawn. However, you can reassure them that you are enlightened, following Nature's way and that Nature knows best.

Safety first

Good diet and good health go hand-in-hand, although accidents can happen.

Dogs, in their enthusiasm to grab a meaty morsel, can bite the hand that feeds them. Most carnivorous animals will 'guard' their natural food. We need to take sensible precautions and avoid teasing the animals. Young children are less able to read warning signals and should never be allowed to disturb feeding pets.

No matter the size of your dog, if it bites it can do harm. My own dogs know not to threaten me and accept that they must give up their food at times of my choosing. Start your young puppies early and you should experience little difficulty training them to both receive and relinquish their food. But if you own a large, dominant or aggressive dog then take extra care. Professional dog trainers can advise.

Whether you feed your animals together or separately depends on personal preference and temperament of your pets. If in doubt, feed animals separately. Cats can be fed on a table top whilst your dogs eat on the floor beneath.

Sources of supply

Old Mother Hubbard went to the cupboard,
To fetch her poor dog a bone;
When she got there, the cupboard was bare,
And so the poor dog had none.

We should be grateful to Mother Hubbard. Learning from mistakes, especially if those mistakes are made by others, is one of the easiest ways to learn.

By planning ahead we can ensure our refrigerator/freezer is never bare. The question remains: Where to find a regular, dependable source of supplies?

Human food outlets

If you buy meat for the family you will already have a fair idea where to pick up raw meaty bones for your pets. Supermarkets, butchers, chicken shops, fish shops, and farmers' markets are the most common sources. You may need to make enquiries if you are looking for larger, meaty bones, pigs' heads and 'unusual' items. Unleash your ingenuity and you may be surprised by what you can find. 'Ethnic' butchers may have sheep's heads, quail, rabbit and other less common delicacies. Let your fingers do the walking and use the *Yellow Pages* to establish leads.

The secret to obtaining regular supplies depends on a good relationship with your meat supplier. If your butcher knows you are a regular customer for whole ox tails he can order stocks to suit. If your chicken shop knows you will call in regularly for chicken backs and frames then these can be saved specially for you.

It's a good idea to exchange information with other raw feeders. By increasing the trade in raw food and developing the market, raw food outlets gain an incentive to order in bulk and keep prices affordable.

(Regulations governing the supply of raw meat, bones and offal vary. Please see Information Resources page 99.)

Bulk supplies

When you get serious and want to buy in bulk then you may need to travel further afield. There are various possibilities. Abattoirs and meat packing plants are good sources of raw meaty bones and offal from beef, pig, sheep and deer. In some districts ostrich, emu and buffalo parts can be obtained from the meat processors.

Chicken processors are an excellent source of backs and frames, wings and necks and sometimes you can obtain 'seconds' stock too.

Informal buyers' co-ops sprang up in North America and now the idea is catching on in the UK and Europe too.

Members place telephone or email orders with a volunteer coordinator. Bulk supplies are delivered to a central location for collection by the co-op members. Besides the usual chicken backs and frames and other raw meaty bones, co-ops deal in whole rabbits, game hens, goats and emu. Mostly the products are frozen and some items may be packed in dry ice and air freighted great distances.

Specialty suppliers, pet shops

Specialty pet-food outlets, whether wholesale or retail, advertise their range of raw meaty bones, offal and whole carcasses. You can find contact details in the *Yellow Pages*, by doing an internet search or posting an enquiry on the Carnivore Suppliers internet list. Internet raw feeding discussion lists are also good sources of information: www.rawmeatybones.com

Some wholesalers and pet shops supply frozen mice, rats and day-old chicks for feeding to reptiles and birds of prey. Increasingly dog, cat and ferret owners are using the same outlets. Home delivery is often part of the service provided by specialty pet-food suppliers.

Zoos and research laboratories

Zoos and research laboratories often have need of large supplies of whole raw carcasses. It's worth a phone call to ask if they would mind sharing their sources.

Sometimes laboratories, for instance university research laboratories, can be a source of rats, rabbits and similar items surplus to their needs.

Zoos may keep colonies of breeding animals as a source of supply for their carnivores. Some pet owners follow the example by raising rabbits, guinea pigs, goats and chickens to feed to their pets.

Ingenuity, innovation and entrepreneurial flair

Hunters, fishermen and farmers frequently have access to good supplies of carcasses and raw meaty bones. In North America, during the deer hunting season, many dog owners stock up on raw, meaty deer bones and heads at bargain prices. If you live in the country or travel on country roads then you may have access to road kill. Providing local laws permit, carry an old cooler-box or plastic sheet to take advantage of the fresh carcasses you find along the way.

Zoos obtain injured and old farm animals unsuitable for human consumption. That's an option for dog owners with large kennels and plenty of freezer space. I know of one zoo that places newspaper advertisements seeking supplies of wild pigeons, squirrels and rabbits. It's stipulated that the animals must either be trapped or killed with steel shot as opposed to the more common lead shot.

With a little ingenuity and innovation you are sure to be able to source good food for your dogs. What starts as a hobby could grow to become a business. If you have entrepreneurial flair you may wish to join the ranks of those who breed prey animals, and supply carcasses and raw meaty bones. Here's wishing you every success.

4

Switching, grinding, breeding

Switching to raw food

Feeding raw meaty bones works wonders for the health of dogs. But getting started, overcoming your fears can be a trifle unnerving. We've all heard the bad press about dogs choking on bones, the vet bills associated with the perforation of a dog's bowel and the nasty bacteria said to lurk in every mouthful of raw food. We don't want to do our pets even the slightest harm. Besides we have a self-image to preserve. We don't want to appear reckless, flouting conventions and open to ridicule.

Relax, wipe the sweat from your brow and dry your palms. Switching your pet's diet is the most important thing you can do to promote health, vitality and longevity. Happily most dogs are in touch with their inner wolf and seize on the first juicy bone you offer. Some dogs, though, addicted to the commercial offerings, may take a bit of persuading.

Let's assume your dog is relatively young, has no major/painful problems with teeth and gums (see Chapter 7) and hitherto has been fed a commercial or home cooked diet. The first question then becomes: Do you introduce changes gradually or switch the diet abruptly?

I recommend that, if possible, you make a complete change without any lead-up. Simply stop the old diet and start the new. At first it's best to choose and stick with one food type until the changeover has been completed successfully. Whole chickens or chicken backs and frames make a good initial meal for all sizes of dog. Simply throw the items on the ground and watch your pet sniff, lick and finally seize the morsels. You may feel the urge to hover for the first few feeding sessions. Try to hover at a distance and so avoid crowding your pet.

After about a week feeding chicken or other chosen food, and providing there are no digestive upsets, you can introduce a variety of other large raw meaty bones and carcasses. Allow a week or so to introduce each new food item before moving on to the next.

What if your dog has become addicted to junk food and you have become habituated to feeding the addiction? Often a 24-hour fast makes a big difference. Resist the temptation to provide a snack of kibble or canned mush. Simply remove all food for 24 hours. The next day, your somewhat confused and hungry pet will be more willing to investigate the strange new offering. If this strategy fails we need to think again.

Switching fussy dogs

For some people the smell, even the thought, of certain foods turns the stomach. Food aversion affects dogs too. For instance if a dog is stung by a bee as he or she eats a chicken carcass or suffers stomach pains associated with a meal of chicken, then aversion to chicken may result. Generally, though, it's not a bad experience but lack of experience that makes dogs refuse new tastes and textures.

Switching the diet of fussy dogs may take a bit of ingenuity using a combination of methods. Like wolves, dogs cope with hunger surprisingly well. It's not unkind to let hunger be your principal tool. Fat dogs can be fasted for lengthy periods without ill effect—even several weeks.[1] Lean dogs can go without food for long periods too. But two or three days of no rations usually works just fine. If the chicken frames are not eaten after an hour, simply return them to the refrigerator until the next day. By the third day your hungry hound will be following your every move—and be a willing participant in the experiment.

Does your dog come to the rattle of dry kibble? Does your dog like to catch tasty morsels, or retrieve the ball? A little teasing and deception, for honorable reasons, may do the trick. Rattle the bowl, but toss small pieces of meat instead. You might try chopping some chicken meat and mixing it with familiar food; gradually increasing the proportions of chicken over a few days and then substituting with large pieces of chicken on the bone. You might try smearing canned food or crushed kibble onto raw meaty bones.

Do you have a small dog that you feed cooked human food? Some small dogs may need their chicken *lightly* grilled. After an introductory period grill the meat less to the point where it's completely raw. Once your dog gets the idea that raw meat tastes good he or she will soon delight in ripping meat and crunching bones. Persistence pays. Do not give up on small dogs. Raw food is essential for them. They need more tooth cleaning, not less.

Once a dog relishes the taste of raw chicken graduating to other raw meaty bones and offal is usually straightforward. However, if a new item creates resistance then try a day or two of fasting. I wish you luck and mention a couple of exceptions— raw feeding is not a mechanical process, we need to stay in touch with the realities of Nature. There are dogs that would rather starve than eat what is otherwise wholesome natural food.

Some dogs relish raw fish and some dogs refuse to eat fish however hard you try. My own dogs eat chicken backs and frames with gusto. But much to my chagrin, when I bought some old laying-hens, with the intention of feeding them warm, feathers, guts and all, the dogs seized the newly-killed hens with a vigorous shake—they made sure the hens were dead, but flatly refused to eat them. I tried plucking the hens; dismembering them; I tried everything I could think of, but still the hens went uneaten. Such is a life with dogs.

The remaining hens lived happily ever after and laid lots of eggs to prove it.

Grinding food, is it necessary?

By ripping and tearing at food carnivores keep periodontal and associated diseases at bay. Take away the tooth cleaning function and you take away a major benefit of raw food. You wouldn't buy watered down medicine, at inflated prices, for your children and similarly it's not good policy to 'water down' the medicinal benefits of raw food.

But seeing as though we are dealing with complex biological systems then very occasionally we need to modify the rules. For short periods of time carnivores can survive perfectly well without bone in the diet. So if a pet is too young or too sick to eat whole raw meaty bones, then the answer is simple—feed chopped or ground meat and offal. (But remember, for a short period of time only.)

Before three weeks of age puppies do not need solids and after six weeks of age they have teeth for ripping and tearing whole food. During the transitional phase from milk to whole food feeding, wolf mothers regurgitate part-digested stomach contents for their puppies. Only a few domestic dogs regurgitate food in this way. If a dog has plenty of milk and the litter is small then supplementary feeding may not be necessary. However, if in doubt provide chopped or ground raw meat along with chicken pieces. By six weeks of age most puppies show a preference for food requiring ripping and tearing and feeding ground food should be discontinued.

For longer term feeding the old and toothless may need their food ground. But I say 'may need'. Even toothless or nearly toothless dogs manage to gum their way through chicken frames. They benefit from the mental and physical exercise and tone the gums. Perhaps in the last few weeks of life an elderly pet may need assistance with eating. Ground or chopped meat and offal work well. At that late stage in life, and for a short period, strict adherence to the need for bone in the diet can be relaxed.

So when do adult dogs need ground raw meaty bones? There is one rare medical condition, megaesophagus, which affects an animal's ability to deliver food to the stomach with resultant pooling of food in the esophagus.[2] Finely ground food must be offered. A rare condition of dogs, pyloric stenosis, may prevent food from passing from the stomach to the small intestine.[3] An operation can usually resolve the problem, but until the surgery is performed it's best to grind the food.

Breeding

Let Nature be our guide. Let the breeding season coincide with a good supply of appropriate food. Yes, it's as simple as that. Wild carnivores breed at the same time there's a maximum number of easy-to-catch juveniles of the prey species.

Feed your breeding stock on a diet as close as possible to that Nature intended and they will have optimum fertility, fetuses will be carried to full term and the birth process will be as uncomplicated as can reasonably be expected.

The reasons for this are obvious when we stop to think about it. Healthy males have healthy sperm and healthy females shed healthy eggs. A healthy uterus provides the best environment for growing embryos; strong uterine and abdominal muscles provide the best chance for a trouble free birth.

Breeders report fewer caesarean sections in animals fed raw as opposed to processed diets. Newborn puppies and kittens tend to be slightly smaller but more vigorous than the sleepy offspring of mothers fed processed food. Puppies and kittens suckling vigorously stimulate the milk supply and contraction of the uterus which in turn ensures the wellbeing of the mother. Healthy mothers lick and clean their offspring thus reinforcing the maternal bond and stimulating circulation, respiration and the voiding of urine and feces by the young.

Carnivore mothers 'clean-up' after their offspring. I was intrigued to learn that 'cleaning-up' may continue longer in those litters fed raw food. No bad odors and mess characteristic of the processed-food fed litters.

Three weeks of age is a good time to start puppies on whole pieces of raw food. Chicken backs and frames make a good first choice providing there is plenty of meat attached to the bones. First the young suck then tug at the meat and by six weeks of age expertly crunch on the soft chicken bones. Whole rabbit and fish carcasses are another good source of food for young animals. Please bear in mind that puppies readily take to a variety of different foods. Introduce a range of raw meaty bones and carcasses early and your pets will grow up with wide tastes.

Supplements

Pregnant women are frequently prescribed extra iron and folic acid. But for pregnant carnivores there's no need for extras. Just feed whole carcasses or raw meaty bones and table scraps. In fact supplementing with minerals and vitamins can do harm.

Occasionally orphan puppies need to be fed milk. If you are fortunate you may have access to a foster mother who will accept the orphans as her own. Otherwise there are good artificial milk preparations obtainable from veterinarians and pet shops. Please remember that carnivore mothers lick their offspring which then urinate and defecate directly onto their mother's tongue. It's most important that you mimic the mother's action after feeding sessions. But you needn't use your tongue! I suggest moistened cotton wool or paper towel works well.

As previously mentioned, puppies between the ages of three and six weeks may require supplementary feeding with chopped or ground food. Finely chopped meat from chicken, fish, rabbit or lean beef works well. Throughout the period of supplementary feeding provide a constant supply of carcasses or chicken frames. Once puppies are adept at ripping and tearing then discontinue the ground or chopped meat.

Growing puppies need plenty of calcium in their diet to ensure the growth of strong bones. Offal and large lumps of raw meat, for instance ox-cheek, can be fed in moderation. However these food items contain little calcium. There's no need, and in fact it can be harmful, to provide calcium or vitamin supplements.[4] The best policy is to provide a natural source of calcium: whole carcasses or raw meaty bones.

5

————➤●◄————

Risk management

As a pioneer feeder of natural food you expect the occasional problem. That, after all, is why you are reading this book. You want to know the downside as well as the upside. If raw meaty bones act as food and medicine for dogs; then you want to know about safety aspects and side effects. Like all successful pioneers you know that risks do not deter you, only help you gain a fuller understanding.

Problems, potential or actual, come in two broad categories—biological and man-made.

Biological problems

Raw food comprises a mass of complex nutrients and textures providing intricate nutritional and medicinal benefits. When appropriate raw food meets the complex anatomy and physiology of dogs things usually go well. However, some dogs refuse to eat raw food—a bit like a child refusing medicine. For other dogs, taking their medicine can be associated with unwanted side effects.

Let's take a look at some possible side effects and strategies for avoiding or dealing with them.

Vomiting

Dogs vomit more readily than humans. The loud heaving and smell may not be to your liking but usually you need not be concerned when your pet vomits raw food—and then eats it again. Some dogs eat too quickly and then vomit. The best solution is to offer food in one big piece requiring plenty of ripping and tearing.

Some dogs are either sensitive to or allergic to a particular meat. If your dog consistently vomits beef, make changes; for instance try feeding rabbit, turkey or venison.

Some dogs vomit bile. In general this poses no risk for your dog but, if in doubt, consult your vet.

If your dog vomits and appears unwell it's best to call your vet.

Regurgitating

Eating too quickly or sensitivity to certain foods are reasons why some dogs regurgitate. You may have difficulty distinguishing between regurgitation and vomiting. Your vet can help.

Diarrhea

Diarrhea is defined as 'abnormally frequent intestinal evacuations with more or less fluid stools'. Sometimes diarrhea follows the introduction of and is associated with raw food. Maybe a dog's enzyme systems need time to adjust or maybe it's to do with the population of bowel bacteria that need time to change. Sometimes the diarrhea derives from the pet being exposed to new bacteria for the first time. Usually, diarrhea following introduction of raw food is short lived and resolves itself. Your role is to keep an eye on things to make sure your dog does not look or act unwell and to clean up the mess.

Dietary sensitivity or allergy may be a trigger for diarrhea.

Some dogs, allergic to cooked meats in processed food, eat the same meat *raw* without ill effect.

If a dog occasionally passes soft or loose stools it's seldom a cause for concern. However, if your pet appears unwell, or if stool abnormalities persist, then best to consult your vet.

Choking

Choking occurs when food or other material obstructs the airways. This is an emergency requiring prompt removal of the obstruction. Try to stay calm. If an animal loses consciousness it's safe to reach in and grab the obstructing item. Meaty bones cut too small can lodge across the airways, but so too can kibble, chew toys and plastic bones.

In 2003 Jake, a 10-year-old lion and king of the pride at a New Zealand zoo, died after choking on a chunk of meat. The zoo owner reported: 'Jake leapt into the air when a big chunk of meat struck him on the wrong angle. It went like a bullet down his gullet and got stuck.'[1] Lions and dogs don't need meat in bite size that can be swallowed whole; they need raw meaty bones—in large pieces.

Stuck bones

Raw bones can and do get stuck in the esophagus (food tube between mouth and stomach). But when investigated the reason can usually be traced to bones which are too small. Chicken necks and wings can be 'vacuumed-up' by large dogs and sometimes create blockage. Ox tail or other vertebrae cut too small and with sharp edges get stuck. Sometimes rib bones wedge in the roof of a dog's mouth. Patients paw at their mouths and drool sticky streams of saliva.

Prevention is always better than treatment. Ensure bones are of suitable size and covered in lots of meat.

Constipation

Wolves in the wild and domestic dogs fed whole carcasses pass feces dressed in 'little fur coats' or sprouting feathers from a recent meal. Digestion of natural food is highly effective and if your dog is fed predominantly raw meaty bones then the fecal residue will be about one third that of dogs fed processed food. Passing the small pellets of powdered bone requires effort compared with the sloppy, smelly excrement of kibble-fed dogs. Moderate straining helps tone muscles and evacuate anal glands (two small sacs at the anus). Severe straining signals that your dog may be constipated.

Constipation, providing there is no blockage, can usually be managed by ensuring a diet of whole carcasses, raw bones covered in plenty of meat and a larger proportion of offal. Some owners add cooked pumpkin or other vegetables to the diet. Indigestible vegetable fiber retains water and keeps feces soft. If constipation persists there may be physiological or anatomical problems that require veterinary attention.

Bull terriers and other dogs with powerful jaws sometimes gobble bones without sufficient chewing. The resultant boney fragments move down to the rectum and form an immovable mass. At times like this you need to call the vet. (Prevention, using *meaty* bones in large pieces, is a better option.)

Microbes and parasites

Bacteria

Bacteria—without them life would be very dull; there would be no life at all. Soil bacteria help plants grow. Gut bacteria assist herbivores to digest plants and help carnivores digest herbivores. The waste product of digestion, feces, contains trillions of living bacteria. Sometimes carnivores take a mouthful. It's their way of accessing essential nutrients in the bacterial 'live prey'.

Despite their essential role bacteria suffer from a poor image. It's true some bacteria give rise to diseases, but healthy carnivores generally suffer no ill effects, even when exposed to high levels of harmful bacteria. Nevertheless we should give some thought to the harmful bacteria that may be found in raw food.

Salmonella and *Campylobacter*

Salmonella and *Campylobacter* are common bacteria found in a variety of locations. The municipal pound, boarding kennels and the droppings of wild birds may be sources of infection.[2] Many kibble-fed dogs carry the bacteria. When humans become infected the source may be traced to salad vegetables or the roast chicken served for dinner.[3] It's best to consider all chicken, including chicken for human consumption, as a potential source of harmful bacteria.[4]

Theoretically the very young, the old and those with a reduced immune system are at greatest risk. When pets are first introduced to raw food, especially chicken, they may develop diarrhea. *Salmonella*, whilst often talked about, is seldom a factor. Sometimes, though, the diarrhea is due to contamination of the chicken with *Campylobacter*. *Campylobacter* induced diarrhea can be treated by your veterinarian. Once recovered, dogs are unlikely to suffer from the problem again.

Bacteria in putrid meat

Dogs, like people, enjoy fermented foods. Bones fermented in the garden bed are a firm favorite—with dogs if not with humans. Soil bacteria seldom give rise to health problems. Although rare, the bacteria in putrefying meat can create digestive upset. Decomposing carcasses of chickens and ducks can be a source of botulinum toxin.[5] Sufferers become weak and paralyzed and need urgent veterinary attention.

Salmon poisoning

An unusual microbe, *Neorickettsia helminthoeca*, lives in parasites which live in fresh-water fish along the west coast of North America from San Francisco to Alaska. If dogs eat infected fish they may develop the potentially fatal disease 'salmon poisoning'.[6] Long-time residents of the region know not to feed their dogs raw fresh-water fish. Newcomers need to take note and, if in doubt, obtain further information from local veterinarians.

Aujeszky's disease

Aujeszky's disease is an uncommon viral disease of young pigs. Rarely, dogs living on pig farms may be found dead after contracting the disease.[7] If you are concerned about Aujeszky's I suggest you consult your vet about prevalence in your region. In general, pork neck bones, pigs' trotters and pigs' heads are a safe, economical source of food for dogs.

Protozoa

Toxoplasma

Raw meat, even though passed for human consumption, and the feces of cats, usually kittens, can be a source of *Toxoplasma* infection—for you and your dog.[8] Because of risks to unborn babies, pregnant women are encouraged to take extra precautions when handling raw meat or cleaning the cat litter tray. Freezing meat at -10 °C kills *Toxoplasma* organisms.[9]

For more information consult your doctor, library or internet.

Neospora

Neospora caninum is an uncommon protozoal parasite of dogs. Puppies may be aborted or develop progressive paralysis. Current opinion is that females consume infected meat and pass on the parasite to the fetuses in the uterus. Freezing meat at -20°C for one day kills *Neospora*.[10]

Sarcocystis

Dogs seldom suffer any ill effects from consuming *Sarcocystis* infected meat. Diarrhea and vomiting may occur.[11] Humans who handle raw beef or pork may become infected. Good meat handling and hygiene recommendations apply.

Worms

If dogs eat their natural raw diet of meat, fish and bones they are likely to contract parasitic tapeworms. Some round worms can also be transmitted to dogs via small rodents. However, in the domestic situation there is no cause for alarm. Raw meaty bones cleared for human consumption contain few if any worm cysts. Similarly, low numbers of adult worms do not create health problems for carnivores. The few worms that do develop can be controlled by regular use of modern worming medicines. And daily removal of feces helps to limit the spread of worm eggs.

Hydatid tapeworm

The hydatid tapeworm *Echinococcus granulosus* needs mention, not because of its effects on dogs but for the potential dangers it poses for humans.

The adult worms are tiny and live in the intestines of domestic dogs, dingoes, wolves, coyotes, jackals and foxes. As with other tapeworms the eggs are passed in the feces and scattered on the herbage. If those eggs are eaten by a suitable intermediate host, for instance a sheep, kangaroo or deer, the eggs hatch into larvae which proceed to the lungs or liver and occasionally other organs. A hydatid cyst develops. It's this cyst, when eaten by a dog or other canine, which develops into the adult worm.

In Australia and the United Kingdom dogs are usually the primary and sheep the secondary hosts. Other strains include a wolf/moose strain in North America, dingo/wallaby strain in Australia, coyote/deer in California and fox/hare in Argentina. Providing the worm stays in those hosts there are few problems. The situation changes if worm eggs find their way into a human and develop into a hydatid cyst. The cysts, if located in an important organ, such as the heart or brain, can have fatal consequences.[12]

How do hydatid tapeworm eggs get into a human? Mostly they come from an infected domestic dog. The eggs are slightly sticky and adhere to the coat of the dog. Transfer to a human, more commonly a child, occurs if the dog licks itself and then the person. Petting a dog, getting worm eggs on fingers and then handling food or sucking fingers achieves the same outcome.

How do domestic dogs become infected? *Not* by eating raw meaty bones purchased from the butcher—meat passed for human consumption poses little or no threat. They become infected by scavenging on sheep and wallaby carcasses found dead in the paddock. Some farmers slaughter sheep for home consumption without checking the offal for signs of hydatid cysts.[13] If infected offal is fed to farm dogs, or city dogs spending time on the farm, then they may become infected. Generally, however, hydatid problems are restricted to rural dogs living in well-known rural areas. Local veterinarians can advise, whether for farm dogs or visitors, regarding prevention and treatment of hydatid disease.

Man-made problems
Raw meaty bones and table scraps—potential problems

It's possible to have too much of a good thing—especially when a pair of imploring eyes beg for more. Some people feed an excess of minced meat without bone and others feed excess amounts of starchy foods and vegetables. Theoretically it's possible to feed too much liver and create vitamin A excess problems.

Too much raw white of egg can reduce the amount of biotin (a B group vitamin) available for your dog. Who feeds lashings of egg white? I've never met such a person. And in any case raw egg yolks contain lots of biotin which mostly compensates for any losses. A steady diet of some fish, for instance carp and herring, can lead to a reduction in vitamin B1. Too much oily fish can give rise to fatty acid excess.

Veterinary teaching and pet-food company marketing have, for many years, been directed against table scraps and created unnecessary alarm. Table scraps, both cooked and raw, can provide welcome calories, trace elements and micronutrients for dogs, but there are a few things to watch out for.

Items to avoid:
- excessive meat off the bone—not balanced
- excessive vegetables—not balanced
- small pieces of bone—can be swallowed whole and get stuck

- cooked bones—can get stuck.
- excessive starchy food e.g. potatoes and bread—associated with bloat
- onions and garlic—toxic to pets and can produce anemia
- fruit pits (stones) and corn cobs—get stuck in the bowel
- milk—associated with diarrhea; animals drink it whether thirsty or not and consequently get fat; milk sludge sticks to teeth and gums
- chocolate—toxic for dogs (beware at Easter and Christmas; keep chocolate away from curious canines)
- mineral and vitamin additives—create imbalance

Cooked products claiming to be 'natural'

Oft repeated propaganda takes hold in people's minds, hence the repetition of the word 'natural' in processed pet-food ads. No matter that grains are not a 'natural' part of a dog's diet; no matter that cooking and pulverizing alters the nutrients and destroys the texture of natural food.

Fad diet books for dogs list so called natural ingredients— grains, vegetables and minced meat—which you are then told to cook on the kitchen stove. Niche marketers use the same confused and misleading concepts to sell their 'premium' cooked products. 'Human-grade ingredients selected and mixed according to a special recipe', they say. 'Cooked and sealed in the bag for your convenience.' If dogs could talk, what would *they* say?

Raw products claiming to be 'natural'

These days, alongside the cooked commercial products there's a wide range of raw pet-food recipes and niche products generally marketed as 'barf', a colloquial term for vomit. 'Barf' proponents dispute that dogs are carnivores. Instead they claim dogs are 'omnivores' and, according to them, should consume large quantities of vegetables and fruit. Several companies manufacture ground meat, bone and vegetables to a 'barf' formula. One 'barf' advertisement claims: 'Quite possibly ... the world's perfect food for your pet!'[14]

Dogs in the wild don't read raw diet ads or spend much time in the vegetable patch. They are too busy catching and consuming prey animals. Ripping and tearing at whole carcasses provides wild dogs with the full medicinal effects of 'tooth brushing' and 'flossing' at *every* feeding session. Pity the pet dogs fed ground raw concoctions—no teeth cleaning for them. Pity the dog owners who swallow the 'omnivore' marketing hype.

Dietary supplements

It's often quipped that expensive vitamin supplements make for expensive urine—excess water soluble vitamins pass out through the kidneys. Are there other costs? In my opinion, yes!

If a diet is thought to be inadequate I recommend that the principal items of the diet be changed. Attempts at finding a suitable artificial supplement to plug nutritional gaps presupposes you know what the gaps are, how wide and how deep. Let's face it; most of us feed ourselves and our families on good food for *all* our nutrient requirements. Why is it that, when it comes to dietary supplements for dogs, we succumb to marketing hype?

Marketers sell flaxseed (linseed) oil, kelp and cider vinegar for their alleged nutrient properties. How does anyone know if their dog suffers a flaxseed oil deficiency? Especially since flaxseed forms no part of a wild dog's diet.

Some people feed raw food to their dogs and then supplement with glucosamine and chondroitin for joint repair

—little realizing that raw meaty bones contain an abundance of glucosamine and chondroitin.[15] A diet of raw carcasses or raw meaty bones provides a good balance of calcium, phosphorous and vitamin D. By adding supplements it's possible to do harm by giving too much calcium and vitamin D, especially to growing pups.

We know that junk food manufacturers strive to identify and plug nutritional gaps in their products with additives and supplements. For us, rather than gain a false sense of security with bottled supplements, it is much better to follow Nature's lead.

Bogus problems

Old-wives tales and other scare stories abound. We've all heard the statements:

- Never feed chicken or fish to dogs—the bones are dangerous.
- Feeding raw meat to dogs gives them a blood lust.
- If you feed lamb to dogs they will chase the farmer's sheep.

In response:

- Cooked chicken and fish bones may be dangerous. Feed only *raw* chicken or fish.
- All dogs, potentially, can inflict a nasty bite. A small minority, when fed a natural diet, become more dominant and aggressive. However, most dogs fed raw food tend to be calm and placid by comparison with those fed junk food.
- Many working sheep dogs are fed sheep offal; dogs on pig farms scavenge dead piglets; packs of foxhounds are fed whole carcasses of farm animals. Working dogs do not harm

the farm animals and even fox hounds ignore the farmer's flock of sheep as they pursue the fox they will not eat.

Sometimes family and friends tell scare stories with the best of intentions. Often it's people with commercial interests who raise hypothetical and bogus concerns. Vets repeat pet-food industry propaganda. How often have you heard the statement: 'Only scientifically produced packaged foods provide a complete and balanced diet?' As a reader of this book you know to be on your guard. You can weed out the half-truths and scare stories before they take root.

6

Nasty diseases

"What did they live on?" said Alice, who always took a great interest in questions of eating and drinking.

"They lived on treacle," said the Dormouse, after thinking a minute or two.

"They couldn't have done that, you know," Alice gently remarked; "they'd have been ill."

"So they were," said the Dormouse; "very ill."

Alice's Adventures in Wonderland, Lewis Carroll[1]

'The results for your liver are obscene beyond anything I would have thought . . . My advice to you as a physician is that you have got to stop' advised Morgan Spurlock's doctor. In the film *Super Size Me*, Morgan Spurlock conducted an experiment. He ate McDonald's meals three times a day for 30 days; ate super-size helpings whenever offered that option; and visited his doctor for regular health checks. Over the 30 days Spurlock became progressively sicker; gained 24 and a half pounds (eleven kilos); his liver turned to fat; cholesterol shot up; and he doubled his risk of heart failure.[2]

Spurlock's doctor had no difficulty making the connection. His patient was becoming seriously ill as a result of a constant junk food diet. The consequences for dogs fed junk food, usually for a lot longer than 30 days, are the same or worse. Happily, just stopping the junk food usually works wonders. Why is this?

Whenever we stop doing harm, we take the first step towards doing some good. And junk foods harm the health of a majority of the world's pet dogs in broadly three, sometimes five, different ways.

1. Soft canned foods and grain-based kibble do not clean teeth. In fact food sludge sticks to teeth and feeds oral bacteria. The result: sore gums, bad breath and bacterial poisons that affect the rest of the body.

2. Dogs don't have the digestive enzymes in the right quality or quantity to deal with the nutrients in grains and other plant material—whether those materials are raw or cooked. When grains are cooked at high temperatures at the pet-food factory the starches, proteins and fats become denatured or toxic in variable degrees. Once in the bowel of a dog, toxic nutrients are absorbed into the circulation and affect various body systems.

3. Poorly digested grain-based junk food supports a large population of toxin-producing bacteria in the lower bowel. The bowel lining, in constant contact with poisons, may be adversely affected. Some poisons pass through the bowel wall into the blood circulation, are carried to other organs and create further problems.

4. Like Morgan Spurlock, some pets show signs of ill health after a short time consuming junk food. For instance,

young puppies frequently suffer from bad skin and diarrhea. Long term exposure to the diet-related toxins listed in 1, 2 and 3 lead to diseases of body organs. Diseased organs produce more toxins which enter the blood stream and add to the toxic load affecting all other organs.

5. Pets affected by the above four categories of poison frequently get taken to the vet. Some vets say: Stop! Stop feeding junk food. Sadly, though, most vets ignore categories 1, 2 and 3. Instead they diagnose diseased organs as mentioned in 4. Treatment usually involves strong pharmaceuticals which then contribute another level of toxic insult.

At the veterinary school, and for the first fifteen years of my life as a qualified vet, I too overlooked the poisons listed in categories 1, 2 and 3. What pets were fed scarcely entered my thoughts. I did work diligently to diagnose and treat diseased organs. And I prescribed lots of pharmaceuticals. When, finally, I awoke to my shortcomings I was aghast and deeply ashamed of my previous failure to help patients under my care.

Once awake to the problems, solutions became obvious. First, stop feeding junk food; second, ensure teeth and gums are healthy; third, if necessary, diagnose and treat diseased organs. I say 'if necessary' for once the junk food is stopped and teeth and gums are restored to health many patients need no further treatment.

Body systems affected by diet
Hair and skin

Have you ever patted a dog and then needed to wash your hands to remove the greasy smell? Do dogs you know, no matter how often they go to the dog-groomer, still give off a fusty odor?

Healthy hair growth depends on the right balance of dietary amino acids, minerals and vitamins. Healthy hair also depends on a healthy skin, healthy immune system and internal organs. If any of these factors are missing or out of balance then brittle, sparse or lusterless hair may result.

A dog's skin is its largest organ and dependent on the good health of other organs of the body—which in turn are dependent on a healthy diet. Fleas, lice and mange mites live on or in the skin. But if a dog's diet is healthy those parasites seem not to create much of a problem. Remarkable stories abound of dogs being diagnosed with 'incurable' flea allergy or demodectic mange. Once those dogs have a change of diet their problems diminish, even disappear. Raw meaty bones work wonders where gallons of insecticide, medicated shampoo and corticosteroids do nothing or do harm.

Ears and eyes

'After trying many failed remedies our dog's ear problems cleared up once we changed his diet' say scores of delighted owners. Others comment on how their dog's previously dull, sad eyes regained a sparkle once the diet was changed. Apart from the need to relieve discomfort it's important to get a dog's sore ears treated effectively and early. Otherwise, a ruptured ear drum and major surgery may be the unfortunate end result.

Nose

'I've got a complaint. I've been feeding my dog raw meaty bones for two years now, and his nose is permanently wet and icy cold. You don't want THAT in your ear when you're having a nap on the sofa … I blame the bones for his superb health and fitness' joked a happy dog owner.

Joking aside, we need a dog's nose to work effectively—especially noses of police dogs, hunting dogs, and bomb detector dogs. Research shows that dogs with a build-up of tartar on their teeth—and that's the majority of dogs fed junk food—have a reduced ability to detect odors.[3] This reduced ability, when coupled with the fact that such dogs have a reduced overall health and fitness, could have disastrous consequences.

Mouth

Dogs fed junk food may be less able to detect odors but they sure generate plenty. 'Dog breath' describes the bad smell wafting off the diseased teeth and sore gums of dogs fed processed food and ground raw products. Pet-food companies acknowledge that 80% of dogs over the age of three years—increasing to 100% of dogs over twelve years of age—suffer from gum disease.[4] Gum disease can affect the liver, kidneys and immune system—often with fatal consequences.[5]

Digestive tract

Anywhere from the mouth to the anus, nasty diseases occur as a result of a junk food diet. According to the Mars Corporation, the world's largest pet-food maker, it's estimated that 10 – 15% of dogs suffer from vomiting and diarrhea.[6] Many dogs suffer from incurable, chronic, inflammatory bowel disease as a direct result of their diet. Every year thousands of dogs die an agonizing death from bloat, where the stomach fills with gas and twists.[7] Dogs fed a natural diet are much less likely to suffer from bloat.[8]

Dogs fed junk food are prone to unsocial habits. If fusty dog skin and dog breath make your nose wrinkle, then junk food farts will affect your nose and make your eyes water too.

Then there's the habit of many dogs that are fed junk food—eating their own poop. Although distasteful to us, many dogs relish the excrement of cows and sheep as a source of vitamins and the bodies of billions of microbes. Dog poop resulting from grain-based junk food is in the same category: copious, sloppy and teeming with 'live prey'. Will TV advertisements show that many dogs prefer their junk food steaming and hot the second time through?

Dogs fed raw meaty bones seldom if ever eat their own excrement. Natural food is well digested the first time. The extra effort required to pass the small, firm stools helps to keep anal glands healthy too.

Liver

Morgan Spurlock's doctor kept a check on Spurlock's liver function during the 30 days he ate McDonald's meals. Unfortunately for dogs, liver tests often fail to reveal damage until it's too late. Liver tests are often not performed and, if they are performed, vets seldom consider diet as the trigger for liver disease.

Pancreas

Like the liver, the pancreas, source of digestive enzymes, has to work excessively hard when dogs are fed cooked junk food. When the pancreas can't keep up with the demand for enzymes, food does not get digested; the dog produces large amounts of excrement whilst becoming thinner and thinner.[9] Most vets keep their pancreas patients on junk food and prescribe pancreatic-enzyme pills and powders. Better if they prescribed a raw diet with plenty of ox or pig pancreas included.

Diabetes mellitus, the inability to regulate blood sugar, is on the increase. Either the pancreas does not produce enough insulin or the insulin produced does not work effectively. Mainstream vets are starting to recognize that high grain-based diets make insulin dependency worse and prescribe less grain and more protein in the diet.[10] But it's not just a matter of reducing carbohydrate levels. Human dentists and doctors recognize that diabetic patients with gum disease frequently have an increased need for insulin. When the patient's gums are treated their insulin needs decline.[11]

A raw meaty bones or carcass-based diet contains little or no carbohydrate and, by cleaning the teeth, keeps gum disease at bay. That seems to be the best way to keep diabetes under control or better still, prevented before it takes hold.

Kidneys

Kidneys work in conjunction with other organs to regulate water levels, filter the blood, and assist with blood pressure maintenance and production of red blood cells. Dogs need healthy kidneys. As with other organs the kidneys have spare capacity; so even though two-thirds of the kidneys may be damaged, the damage may not be obvious without specialized tests.[12] If and when tests are performed and kidneys are found to be failing, many vets fail to consider the prime reasons—a diet of junk food and periodontal disease.

Lungs, heart and blood vessels

The full extent of junk food damage to the lungs, heart and blood vessels in dogs is yet to be explored. In humans it's well known that nutrients in junk foods affect the heart. Doctors and dentists increasingly warn that chronic gum disease can trigger heart attacks, lung disease and stroke.[13] Some vets sound similar warnings.

Musculoskeletal system

Have you seen old dogs dawdling behind their owners in the park?—tired, stiff gait and weary look in the eye. They are the poor unfortunates ground down by a lifetime consuming junk food. If only we knew how much their muscles and joints ache! Take those same old, worn out dogs and change their diets; treat their gum disease and oftentimes they become 'like puppies again'—no further need for expensive visits to the vet, assorted pills and supplements.

Brain

Diet-related brain disease, whether mild or severe, is often misdiagnosed, mistreated and fatal.

Perhaps we should not be surprised if young dogs, whose brains are bombarded with strange dietary chemicals and immune disturbances, suffer from headaches, irritability and poor attention spans. Professional dog trainers tell me that delinquent behavior frequently disappears and dogs become easy to train when owners change over to natural feeding.

Some dogs fed junk food suffer from epileptic seizures; others fly into unpredictable rage and attack their owners.[14, 15] When conventional treatments fail, whether for delinquency or severe brain disease, many dogs receive a final, fatal injection. A change of diet may be a better option.

Immune system

The immune system, when healthy and working well, helps repair and recycle worn and damaged body parts. Through an elaborate system of cells, antibodies and messenger chemicals, the immune system monitors the body for invading microbes and cancer.

Failure of the immune system takes many forms and varies from the mild to the severe, the chronic to the acute. Immune failure is often the result of a junk food diet. When we have fuller, objective research we shall learn the extent to which diet affects the immune system. It may be that junk food manufacturers already know and are not telling—except where it helps their marketing strategies. Junk food manufacturers fortify their products with antioxidants because, they say, it helps puppies develop a better immune response to vaccinations.[16] They make claims for products said to combat arthritis, gum disease and the effects of aging—in other words they acknowledge diet affects the immune system.

Thousands, perhaps millions, of dogs are diagnosed with skin allergy and inflamed bowels. They receive tons of corticosteroids and other toxic drugs when a change of diet may be the only 'treatment' required. Allergy or hyperactivity of the immune system can lead to the immune system attacking the body, often with severe, even fatal consequences. Sometimes, though, after years of fighting valiantly, the immune system collapses. I investigated a number of dogs suffering from immune depression and severe gum disease after a lifetime of eating junk food. When the gum disease was treated and the diet changed the dogs became like new.[17]

Whole body

When we take account that all body parts are connected, and that the whole is greater than the sum of the parts, then we can understand that a good diet is essential for overall good health.

Some dogs fed on junk food are painfully thin, but many are overweight or obese. For both groups of dogs a change of diet is often the only change necessary for them to regain good shape and good health.

Dogs fed junk food are prone to infections with the need for high doses and long courses of antibiotics. Naturally fed animals are less susceptible to infection; they also recover from disease and injury quicker and with less need for toxic drugs.

We need more information about the cancer epidemic in domestic dogs. However, basic nutritional and medical principles tell us that diet is the likely main factor.[18] Without waiting for extra information, and because cancer often takes years to develop, it's best to start puppies on a cancer prevention diet early—even before birth.

Breeders tell me that puppies are born stronger and the need for caesarean delivery decreases when bitches are fed a natural diet. If puppies are weaned to natural food and then fed natural food for life, how much longer can they expect to live compared with dogs fed a commercial diet? Currently we lack an answer; we need more research. We do know that many, perhaps a majority, of animals fed junk food live miserable lives and die a long, slow death. By contrast dogs fed a natural diet live more comfortable, disease-free lives and when the end comes tend to have a shorter period of infirmity. From the whelping box to the grave let 'prevention not treatment' be our motto.

7

Dentistry matters

Imagine eating nothing but canned stew or kibble every day of your life without ever brushing your teeth—or perhaps once in a while having a toothbrush thrust in your mouth by a concerned friend. Can you imagine your dentist selling cans of stew and bags of kibble?—telling you that the products are the best and most scientific that money can buy. Would human dentists promote carrot-shaped chews and plastic apples as tooth cleaning aids for children and adults? For dogs, it's part of their reality in the modern artificial pet-food world—except of course, the dental chews and plastic toys sold by doggy dentists, veterinarians, are bone-*shaped*.

Dogs' reality is worse still when you consider that the majority of veterinarians not only push artificial bones but simultaneously demonize the real thing. According to a 2003 British Small Animal Veterinary Association 'health-care' booklet:

> Puppies and dogs love chewing bones, but sadly they often lead to a trip to the vet's surgery, because the dog has swallowed a sharp fragment, cut his mouth or broken a tooth. A better idea is to give your pet manufactured nutritional chews, or a chew toy, instead.[1]

Clearly then, dogs need friends who understand the essential connection between dogs and bones. And, for the foreseeable future, dogs need owners to wrest back control of their dogs' dental care.

Please use this chapter to 'bone up' on dentistry for dogs. You don't need to pass exams, become accredited or buy expensive dental equipment; just learn some basic anatomy, dental disease prevention and control.

Anatomy

Compare the size and shape of the average dog's jaws with your own and straightaway you notice big differences. Relative to the size of its head, a dog's jaws are much larger than a human's jaws. A dog's jaws extend in front of the eyes and are covered by lips like elastic curtains. When the lips are pulled back and the jaws open wide you can see the tools of trade of the carnivore, 42 specialized teeth—some small, some large, and

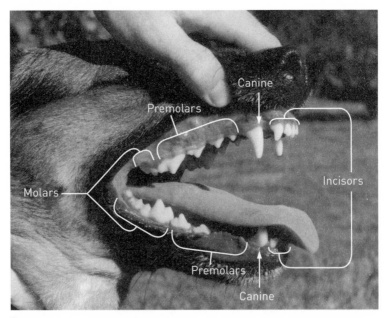

PEARLY WHITES ON DISPLAY
PODGE AGED 3 YEARS

very different from our own.

Twelve incisor teeth nestle in two rows between the four large, dagger-shaped canine teeth. Incisors are used for tugging and nibbling at meat on bone, for holding food, for self-grooming and chasing fleas through the hair coat. Dogs snarl and display canine teeth as a useful reminder of the harm they can inflict; occasionally the teeth are used in a fight. Few domestic dogs use their canine teeth for killing prey. But like wolves in the wild, domestic dogs use canine teeth for raking and tearing meat from bone.

Triangular, knife-like teeth, the premolars, are firm set with gum spaces between. Premolars slice through hide, tendons and meat and shear bones in a scissor-like action. A dog's flat molar teeth are located at the back of the mouth, close to the jaw hinge where, like a nutcracker, maximum forces act to crush meat and bone. If you watch a dog eating a chicken frame he throws the item from side to side, dicing and crushing the food before swallowing in large lumps. Jaws chomp up and down, never side to side like the chewing and grinding action of humans and herbivores such as cows and sheep.

Dogs' teeth have a hollow centre, the root canal or pulp cavity, running from the tip of each root up into the crown of the tooth. Nerves and blood vessels enter the root canal and supply sensation and nourishing blood from within. Incisors and canine teeth have single roots as do small premolar and molar teeth. Other teeth have two or three roots anchored firmly in sockets in the jaws.

Like humans, dogs have a deciduous set of teeth followed by a permanent set. Human deciduous or milk teeth erupt slowly one or two at a time between 6 months and two years of age. Equally slowly we replace our baby teeth with permanent teeth starting at five and a half years of age and ending when we cut our wisdom teeth as young adults.

By comparison puppies cut their full set of deciduous teeth between three and six weeks of age. Between four and six months of age deciduous teeth are shed and simultaneously a new set of permanent teeth appears. (Variations occur.)[2]

At times of teething massive upheavals occur in the gums of dogs. No wonder that puppies like to chew on hard objects to help soothe inflamed gums. And for them, the ideal 'teething ring' is provided by nature—raw meaty bones.

Once adult teeth fully erupt they cease to grow. Despite their tough job they resist wear and tear and last a lifetime. Minerals in saliva maintain and repair shiny tooth surfaces.

Normal inhabitants of the mouth

More than 600 species of bacteria are known to live in the mouths of humans.[3] No one knows for sure how many species live in a dog's mouth. Although you can bet it's a lot. We do know that approximately 300 million individual microbes live in one milligram of dental plaque, the furry coating you find on your teeth each morning.[4] Some plaque bacteria, aerobes, need oxygen and live at the surface of the plaque. Others, anaerobes, hide from oxygen and live deeper in the plaque. Communities of aerobes and anaerobes cooperate, the waste products of one community being food for the other.

From the beginning of life on earth, over three billion years ago, microbes at first clung on to the environment and later changed the environment to suit their purposes.[5] It's the same in the mouths of carnivores (and other animals). The warm, wet environment of the mouth provides specialized niches where bacteria cling—crevices of the tongue, gums and tooth surfaces. If bacteria are left undisturbed they proliferate and set about changing the oral environment to better suit themselves. That's when trouble starts.

Gum disease

In human mouths a build-up of bacteria on teeth surfaces may lead to development of dental caries. Fortunately dogs seldom suffer from caries. They do, however, suffer the ravages of periodontal disease—the foul-smelling disease of the gums and supporting structures of the teeth. Put simply, anything that facilitates the development of bacteria on teeth and gums facilitates the development of periodontal disease.

Minutes after being cleaned from the surface of a tooth, plaque bacteria return. The first arrivals attach sticky glue. More bacteria arrive and soon a sophisticated community develops called a 'biofilm'. Biofilm bacteria live in distinct 'neighborhoods' linked by communication and distribution channels enveloped in protective slime—like the slime on shower curtains and rocks at the seashore.[6]

Within 24 to 48 hours plaque biofilm hardens as minerals in saliva are formed into a tough, protective coating we call calculus or tartar. Living in and on the calculus, biofilm bacteria produce many different chemicals, some potent enough to dissolve living bone and the collagen (tough protein) attachments of teeth.[7] At the line where tooth meets gum a small natural crevice, the gingival sulcus, opens up under the effect of the bacterial colonization. Bacteria, particularly anaerobes, move deeper and deeper into the crevice between tooth and gum.

The body's second line of defense, the immune system, becomes aware of the bacterial invasion and counter attacks with chemical warfare. Damage escalates; gums become red and swollen; body chemicals designed to destroy bacteria damage gum tissue creating further opportunities for the plaque biofilm.[8]

Trapped hair, food debris, misshapen mouths and tooth and

gum injuries—especially when puppies are teething—further assist the invading plaque. It's a vicious cycle. As chemicals and bacteria from diseased gums enter the blood circulation other organs and systems become affected—for instance the kidneys, liver and immune system. Diseased kidneys, liver and immune system contribute to worsening gum disease.

Rotting gums give off the characteristic 'dog breath', but otherwise the septic oozing mess tends to be hidden from view.[9] Dogs with large teeth relative to thin jaws, for instance Toy poodles and Pomeranians, seem especially susceptible. Their gums first swell then recede, the jaw bones dissolve and their teeth fall out.

Prevention

The bad news is that periodontal disease can be hard to detect, even for trained experts. Human dentists refer their patients to specialist periodontists for diagnosis and treatment—and that's for patients who sit still and open wide.

The good news is that you don't need specialist knowledge or training to *prevent* canine periodontal disease. 'Use it or lose it' the saying goes. If your dog's teeth are used as Nature intended, at every feeding session, and from a young age they get the wash, scrub and polish necessary to keep plaque bacteria at bay.

As a note of caution; self-cleaning of teeth occurs best in breeds with mouths resembling those of wolves and dingoes. If dogs' mouths are misshapen, for instance in some toy breeds, in flat faced breeds or those with unusually long narrow faces, then the cleaning process may be inadequate. If teeth are painful or missing or if food is fed ground or in small pieces then the cleaning process will be less effective. Diagnosis and treatment may be required.

Diagnosis

Have a sniff. Does your dog's breath smell fresh, smell rancid or are you not sure? Take care, and without getting bitten, practice sniffing the breath of friendly dogs. Good diagnosticians practice to make perfect.

Visual diagnostic clues range from the subtle to the extreme. Are gums red or swollen? Have gums shrunken from their original line revealing the roots? If your dog has difficulty eating, paws at her mouth and drools saliva she may have a broken tooth, loose teeth or severe periodontal disease. On closer inspection is there build-up of tartar on teeth, or hair or debris stuck in the crevice between teeth and gums?

If in doubt, and at routine veterinary examinations, be sure to ask your vet to make a thorough check. If he/she is in doubt request an examination under general anesthetic. I don't want to be melodramatic about this but, in these days of the junk pet-food cult, most dogs have bad breath and 80% or more of dogs over three years of age have periodontal disease at a level requiring treatment.[10] Vets become so used to seeing oral disease, they either don't notice or they think oral disease is 'normal'.

An extreme example of veterinary oversight involved a 10-year-old Labrador owned by Guide Dogs for the Blind. As a companion dog for elderly people she had regular check-ups at a prestigious veterinary hospital. At the last check-up the vet wrote in the health record book: 'All OK except some tartar developing.' But things were far from OK. In fact both upper and lower jaws were rotting and, when I was called in four months later, 21 teeth needed extraction.[11]

If your vet lacks experience or, for any reason, appears uncertain, it may be wise to seek referral to a specialist veterinary dentist.

Treatment

Tooth cleaning and tooth removal are the two essentials of dental treatment—and very often tooth cleaning is all that's required. Human dentists recommend that patients with bleeding gums spend extra time brushing the teeth and gums.[12] After a week the gums are usually healed. It's the same with dogs. If your dog is relatively young and does not have broken teeth then a few days using Nature's tooth brush, raw carcasses or raw meaty bones, may be the only treatment necessary.

If, for any reason, a change of diet is insufficient to solve the problem, then examination and treatment under anesthesia is the next step. Anesthetics are relatively safe these days, but nonetheless are costly and best avoided. Before giving the OK to your vet, it's best to reach an agreement as to what will happen in the event teeth are found to be loose or seriously diseased and in need of extraction. If possible try to schedule all procedures to be performed under one anesthetic.

'Treat the patient not the tooth' is my motto when deciding whether to clean or extract a tooth. If, by cleaning, a tooth can continue to serve a useful purpose then I clean it. But if a tooth and surrounding gum are likely to be a constant source of periodontal disease poisons and pain for the patient, then I remove the tooth. I recommend that you reach a similar agreement with your vet prior to the commencement of dental treatment.

This point is worth emphasizing because too many veterinarians and veterinary technicians devote effort to polishing dead and diseased teeth that, whilst they may look good immediately after dental treatment, continue to poison the patient—even if the patient is fed a tough, chewy natural diet.

After the patient returns home, in nearly every case, a tough chewy diet, for instance chicken carcasses, pummels and massages sore gums back to good health. Soft diets don't soothe sore gums; in fact they prolong the healing process.

Broken teeth

Teeth break for a variety of reasons and contrary to the scare stories it's seldom due to eating a natural diet. Dogs' canine teeth clash in fights and snap on impact with other hard surfaces. Sometimes premolar and molar teeth split when dogs gnaw 'recreational' bones (large beef marrow bones).[13] Chewing on tennis balls and bricks may expose the pulp cavity. Dogs that constantly chew at the hair coat, mostly as a result of diet-induced skin disease, may abrade teeth down to the pulp cavity too.

Open root canals funnel infection directly into the blood stream. Delaying treatment is not an option. And in my opinion root canal therapy is not a valid option either.

Root canal therapy involves plugging and sealing the tooth and can be counted on to store up trouble. Many root canal treated teeth develop abscesses at the roots and give rise to discomfort and pain.[14] Even treated teeth that remain pain free are likely to continue discharging toxins from the bacteria trapped in the dentine tubules.[15]

If a tooth is broken and the pulp cavity is exposed I recommend, in the best interests of the patient, that the tooth should be extracted.

Puppies

Puppies fed processed food often have septic, foul smelling mouths. Deciduous teeth, which should be shed with ease, hang by shreds of inflamed gum. Happily most puppies quickly take to a healing diet of carcasses or raw meaty bones.

Occasionally deciduous canine teeth persist, firmly anchored in the gums, past the time for shedding at six months of age. If your pup's deciduous canines persist past seven months of age then it's best to have them removed.

Older dogs

When owners consult me about problems affecting their pets I seek to provide answers for their specific concerns. But, consistent with the motto 'treat the patient not the ailment', I include discussion of dietary and dental needs. Ailments are often temporary or of a minor nature—dietary and dental needs are paramount and permanent.

Older dogs frequently suffer from moderate to severe periodontal disease. Once diagnosis is made the question often arises: Is the patient too old to undergo treatment? It's here that medical, emotional and ethical values can collide. Each case needs to be judged on its merits.

The following check list may help you with difficult decisions:

- How severe is the dental disease?
- What investigations need to be performed to obtain fuller information?

- What other medical and surgical conditions affect the patient?
- How much pain/discomfort/suffering is being endured by the patient?
- If untreated, how much longer can the patient be expected to live?
- What is the anesthetic risk?
- What monetary costs are involved?
- What other implications arise if the diseased mouth is left untreated?
- Do you need a second or specialist opinion before taking decisions?

Sometimes, to relieve suffering, it's kindest to administer an overdose of anesthetic and, humanely, euthanase the patient. But in my experience I generally find it's kindest, even in very old dogs, to remove diseased teeth, clean up the mouth and give the patient a new lease of life.

Tooth brushes, dental chews and prescription diets

Canine teeth, which don't get used for gnawing on bones, sometimes accumulate plaque and tartar. Tooth brushing can help. Use a soft human toothbrush or moistened rag in a circular action at the gum margin. Hard deposits may first need to be removed with a dental scraper or other metal instrument. (You may need to consult your vet.)

Sometimes, in dogs with misshapen mouths or missing teeth, tooth brushing can provide an additional aid to teeth cleaning. In general, though, toothbrushes and dental chews represent failed artificial solutions for artificially created problems. Unfortunately too many owners gain a false sense of security by believing the marketing hype. Their pets suffer in silence.

So called recreational bones are frequently promoted by proponents of packaged raw foods. And frequently this adds further injury to insult. Not only do hard indigestible bones fail to clean teeth; oftentimes they break teeth and therefore are best avoided.[16]

Do you believe that anyone would seriously consider cleaning their teeth and gums with wheat cookies (biscuits)? Of course not and it's best not to believe the marketing hype about prescription kibble for dogs either. Insofar as those products remove tartar, it's the tartar on the crowns of the teeth that gets abraded. Down at the gum line, where the bacteria do the damage, the kibble turns to sludge and further feeds the bacteria. By contrast, raw meaty bones scrape, squeegee and polish teeth *and* gums clean.

8

———⟶ ⤜⤜ ⟵———

Sound and vision

The primitive sound of a dog crunching on bones connects with a distant past; it also helps conjure a vision of the future—with immense potential benefits. Let's consider some of the benefits and how we can turn vision into reality.

Wellbeing of the animals

There can be no doubt that carnivores, be they wild or domestic, thrive on the diet prescribed by Nature. Commonsense tells us that, unless traveling on a spacecraft, dogs and all other carnivores should be fed a diet that best caters for their nutritional and medicinal needs. Since nearly all dogs, cats and ferrets and increasing numbers of zoo animals are fed junk food, then the potential for improving the wellbeing of animals is immense.

The rest of our journey starts here. We can start by feeding our own pets the best diet and thus set a good example for others to follow. But we can become more active; we can talk with family and friends and then link up with others through the internet to spread the word to a wider community. Teaching children from kindergarten upwards about carnivore biology will lay the foundations for independent thought, the will and the ability to resist the false messages of the junk pet-food industry. You can start by teaching children or by teaching teachers—getting started is what's important.

Veterinary services

Consider what will happen to the provision of veterinary services when we have a population of healthy dogs and other carnivores. Think of the benefits when trips to the vet become a rarity. Less time, money and effort will be needed to queue at the vets; less time and effort will be spent pushing pills down reluctant gullets; less time, money and effort will be spent on shampoos and flea treatments. With major reductions in need for veterinary treatments the need for veterinary schools and pharmaceutical products will likely fall dramatically.

How then to make this vision a reality when all those with vested interests seek to thwart you? First, know thy enemy. Know that veterinary associations, veterinary schools, junk pet-food makers and pharmaceutical companies want to stop you. Sad to say, government departments, medical and dental research organizations and animal welfare bodies are products of and have a stake in the current system and cannot be counted on for help.

OK, so we have lots of opposition and little or no help. At least we know where we stand. Start by finding a vet who extols the benefits of a whole carcass or raw meaty bones diet. Encourage your friends and neighbors to travel the extra distance to find vets who know and understand the essentials of carnivore nutrition.

Convenience/economy

'Canned and packaged food is so much more convenient' people often remark. *Convenient?* Dogs, if asked, would *not* say it's *convenient* to be fed a harmful diet, to endure repeated trips to the vet, to be permanently bad-tempered and in danger of snapping out of pain and frustration. And, I suspect, owners, once they fully understand the implications won't describe opening a can or packet as *convenient* either. Besides, what's *inconvenient* about stocking a freezer and then throwing frozen raw meaty bones to our pets?

What about the costs? Feeding a harmful junk food diet can hardly be supported because it's allegedly cheaper. In many instances, and depending on where you live, natural food costs less than packaged food. But food costs are only part of the equation. We also need to reckon on the costs of trips to the vet, costs of medications, and the costs of cleaning up piles of offensive smelling dog poop—the natural variety weighs and smells much less. Dogs that are fed junk food tend to be harder to train and more liable to bite their owners.[1] Training costs and medical costs need to be counted too.

Non-monetary costs ought to be considered. Dog owners suffer stress and sometimes a sense of guilt when their pets are repeatedly ill or require early euthanasia.

Then there are the hidden costs borne by taxpayers and the wider community. Taxes pay for veterinary schools that promote pet-food propaganda and for government regulatory departments that are supposed to protect the community but don't. Pet-food advertising is a hidden and substantial cost in the can and packet. Advertisements promote junk pet-food consumption in part by encouraging pet ownership. When a high proportion of pets become unwanted strays the community pays for the municipal pound or welfare society to take care of the problem.

When the convenience and economy myths are better understood the resistance to feeding a more natural diet will likely diminish. We need to do two things. First, stop the myth making by the junk pet-food industry and their allies. Second, train a clear light on the situation; help people see all the convenience myths and explain the costs. Most people, when they experience the benefits themselves, become firm converts.

Environment

These days no new initiative can be approved without passing the environmental impact test. Raw feeding passes the test. The junk pet-food industry fails and is a blight on the natural environment. By limiting the junk pet-food industry we will limit unnecessary processing, packaging and transportation. Land used for cereal crops grown for inclusion in junk pet food can be utilized for other purposes. Rabbits, kangaroos, feral goats and other species well-adapted to the environment can form the basis of a more environmentally sustainable pet-food industry.

When animals are fed a healthy diet there's less need for products of environmentally harmful industries like pharmaceuticals, shampoos and flea treatments. Importantly, public parks and waterways will suffer less dog feces contamination too. Our stewardship of planet Earth requires that we tread lightly. But the polluting pet-food industry monster tramples wherever it goes. When we have full judicial, parliamentary and congressional inquiries the impact of the monster and its protective cordon of professionals will become more widely known. Meanwhile, as concerned citizens, we can start to promote awareness for the sake of dogs and all Earth's inhabitants.

Human health

In subtle and not so subtle ways the junk pet-food industry injures human health. Let's take a look at what's known and in need of attention.

Dog bites

In the USA there are almost 5 million dog bites every year—over 13,000 every day. Extrapolated worldwide that's a considerable problem and for individuals it can be devastating. Children are often victims and often suffer bites to the face. [2]

In almost every case the dog is fed junk food. The question arises: Was the diet the main factor influencing the dog's behavior, a contributory factor or not a factor at all? We can say that dogs fed junk food tend to be excitable and harder to train. One significant trial found some Golden Retrievers, normally a docile breed, attacked their owners when fed junk food, but became docile when fed cooked lamb and rice. [3] How might the dogs have behaved if fed on raw natural food? Objective research is now an urgent priority; thousands of victims every day need answers.

Working dogs

Human health and welfare sometimes depends on dog health—for instance the health of assistance dogs, search and rescue dogs and bomb detection dogs. As we know, dogs fed junk food are seldom truly healthy and consequently perform below par.

Researchers studied a group of beagles that, over a period of months, suffered from a progressive accumulation of dental tartar and simultaneously lost the ability to detect odors. The dogs' teeth were cleaned and within one day their odor detecting abilities returned to normal.[4] Imagine the consequences if a junk-food-fed dog, its teeth encrusted with tartar, failed to detect a terrorist bomb.

Human anxiety

The pet-food industry spends lots of money on advertisements, on university departments and international symposia promoting the unqualified notion that dogs are good for human health and wellbeing. In April 2004 *The Sydney Morning Herald* reported:

> Older Australians who own a pet are more likely to be depressed and in poorer physical health than people who don't own pets, according to a major new Australian study. Flying in the face of claims from the pet-food industry, and others, the study shows pet ownership confers no health benefits to older people.[5]

Could this compromised mental and physical health be due, at least in part, to the ill health of pets maintained on commercial diets? Could it be due to the worry associated with escalating vet bills?

Immune system depression

In 1995 the *Journal of Small Animal Practice*, journal of the British Small Animal Veterinary Association, published results of my research on dogs and cats affected by diet-induced periodontal disease and immune deficiency. By cleaning the teeth and changing the diets the animals' immune systems bounced back to a much healthier state.[6] The implications for immune system research in general, AIDS research in particular and wider aspects of animal and human health are immense.

Rather than promote further inquiry the Editor of the *Journal of Small Animal Practice* bowed to pressure from angry veterinarians and banned discussion within the pages of the *Journal*. The Editor also revoked written undertakings and prevented re-publication of the paper—thus stopping a wider readership from learning about and acting on the implications.[7]

The veterinary research community enjoys many privileges; they also have obligations. When published research challenges established beliefs or has the potential to transform the lives of millions, researchers need to promptly repeat the work to either verify or refute the new information. In 2002, seven years after publication of the original paper, Professor Tony Buffington, a spokesperson for American veterinary researchers, stated: 'I've seen the paper. I haven't seen it reproduced by anyone anywhere else.'[8]

Dogs in medical research

New medical treatments and pharmaceuticals are often tested on dogs before use on humans. Dogs used in medical research are invariably fed junk food. I mentioned to one researcher, who was working on a new anti-inflammatory drug, that most dogs fed commercial food are suffering from gum inflammation (known to be linked to heart disease, stroke, cancer and Alzheimer's) and that my research showed that the so called normal blood values could not be relied upon. He shrugged and said his research team used more dogs in each experiment to help compensate for statistical errors!

Unexplored opportunities

The junk pet-food industry and its allies insist that dogs fed processed food are the healthiest; whereas the opposite is the case. Dogs are subject to a range of illnesses like ourselves— diabetes, arthritis, kidney disease and cancer—and often show dramatic health improvements when switched from junk food to a natural diet. Why *do* previously sick, debilitated animals, in the space of a few days, become 'like puppies again'? The question needs to be asked because the biological mechanisms could have dramatic implications for human diets and health.

There are enough known junk pet-food issues to mobilize an army of medical and dental researchers. Why, then, is more research not performed? For health's sake we must find doctors and dentists who are willing to take the necessary initiatives. Meanwhile we can take steps to improve our own health based on what we know works for dogs. We can start eating a more natural diet and pay special attention to our own dental hygiene. And, rather than treat 'dog breath' as an item of fun, we can use it to teach children the perils of failing to clean teeth.

Science in society

We are supposed to learn from our mistakes and there are few mistakes as big as the junk pet-food debacle. Junk science provides the shaky foundation upon which the entire edifice of the junk pet-food industry is built. Many who administer the system, the so called scientists and regulators, are living a lie. Systems intended to enlarge our understanding of the world and to protect us from exploitation do the opposite.

Our vision has been obscured for too long. We now need major inquiries, with all the legal and political will, with all the legal and political authority, to investigate the debacle and put in place people and systems to carry us forward to a better future. Our dogs live in touch with the teachings of Nature. They cannot tell us in words but, if we allow it, the sound of their crunching raw meaty bones can speak volumes. Let's listen to the sounds of Nature. Let's make a start on a mighty endeavor. It's worth a try; it could work wonders.

INFORMATION RESOURCES

Starting in the 1860s the junk pet-food industry gradually displaced the old, healthy ways of feeding dogs. However, the physical resources and knowledge base for feeding raw food have not been altogether lost, they just need rediscovering.

Local knowledge

Armed with this book and a new resolve you can obtain much useful information in your locality. Butchers, supermarket meat-counter managers and dog clubs can all be valuable sources of information regarding price and availability of food supplies. But take care. Sometimes information may not be accurate. In the wake of the mad cow (BSE) epidemic some European Union butchers believed that new regulations prohibited them from supplying raw bones for dogs. It's true that several countries introduced regulations restricting the supply of bovine heads and spinal tissue although, for dogs, BSE poses no known risk.

Internet

For up-to-the-minute information consult the internet. Search government websites for information on meat, livestock and wildlife regulations. Toll free telephone numbers are often available. Internet discussion lists and raw meaty bones support group websites provide valuable help for beginners. For links and to subscribe to the *Raw Meaty Bones Newsletter* go to

www.rawmeatybones.com

Some support groups provide details of 'raw friendly' vets and raw food outlets. Commercial suppliers of carcasses and raw meaty bones can be found via the search engines.

Feeding the inner wolf

- Make fresh water constantly available.
- Feed whole carcasses of game animals, birds and fish whenever possible.
- Maintain variety in the diet by feeding raw meaty bones from a range of animals.
- Three days each week is a reasonable upper limit for feeding your dog offal.
- Feed table scraps/puréed fruit and vegetable peelings as available.
- Feed one meal daily in one large piece (where possible) to encourage maximum ripping and tearing.
- Dogs can be fed at any time of day. Feeding in the evening works best for most pet owners.
- Many dogs benefit from fasting one day per week.

Two week sample menu

	MON	TUES	WED	THURS	FRI	SAT	SUN
WEEK A	Beef	Fish	Chicken	Lamb	Pig	Chicken	Beef
WEEK B	Chicken	Rabbit	Chicken	Fish	Turkey	Offal	Lamb

SUITABLE CARCASSES AND RAW MEATY BONES

Chicken/poultry Chicken wings can be fed to very small dogs. Chicken frames (minus the meat removed for human consumption) are good for all sizes of dogs. Whole chickens, turkey wings and thighs are suitable for most dogs.

Fish Whole fish, including intestines and scales, and fish heads are suitable for most dogs.

Lamb Large meaty lamb bones, lamb necks, meaty lamb brisket and ribs are good value.

Beef Meaty beef ribs, ox tail in large pieces and ox cheek are suitable for dogs of all sizes.

Pig Pigs' trotters, heads and tails are suitable for most dogs.

Rabbit Feed whole rabbit complete with fur and intestines or skinned and gutted as available. If desired, rabbits can be cut into pieces for very small dogs—although even tiny dogs benefit from tackling whole rabbit carcasses.

Offal Liver of any animal, heart, lungs, spleen, tripe (preferably green unwashed) are suitable for all dogs.

Game animals and birds Feed raw meaty bones and offal from deer, emu, ostrich, kangaroo, etc as available.

QUANTITY

Vary the quantity and size of the pieces according to the appetite, size and weight of your dog. As a guide small dogs tend to eat about 20% of their body weight in raw meaty bones over a one week period. Larger dogs tend to need between 10 and 20% of body weight. Table scraps and fruit can be fed as extra components of the diet.

For fuller details, including feeding puppies, see Chapter 2.

NOTES

Chapter 1
Getting started

1. Engel, C (2003) Food, medicine, and self medication, in *Wild Health: How animals keep themselves well and what we can learn from them*, Phoenix, London p 26

2. Newsome, A E et al (1983) The feeding ecology of the dingo, *Australian Wildlife Research*, 10:3 477–486

3. Lonsdale, T (1995) Periodontal disease and leucopenia, *Journal of Small Animal Practice*, 36, 542–546

4. Mioche, L Bourdiol, P Monier, S (2003) Chewing behaviour and bolus formation during mastication of meat with different textures, *Archives of Oral Biology*, 48(3):193–200

5. Lang, K et al (2003) Neurotransmitters regulate the migration and cytotoxicity in natural killer cells, *Immunology Letters*, 90(2-3):165–72

6. (1996) *Nutrition in Practice*, Edition 3/1996 Uncle Ben's of Australia, Albury Wodonga

7. Burger, I H (1990) Chapter 2, A basic guide to nutrient requirements, in *The Waltham Book of Dog & Cat Nutrition*, 2nd Edition, Ed A T B Edney, Pergamon, Oxford p 13

Chapter 2
Quality, quantity, frequency

1. Hammett, D E and Russell, G S (2005) Species Showcase Rabbit Care, *PetStation*, Web: www.petstation.com/rabbitcare.html

2. Elephant Information Repository (2005) Web: http://elephant.elehost.com/

3. Ask the Meatman (2005) Web: www.askthemeatman.com/how_to_estimate _deer_weights.htm

4. Anson, R M et al (2003) Intermittent fasting dissociates beneficial effects of dietary restriction on glucose metabolism and neuronal resistance to injury from calorie intake, *Proceedings of the National Academy of Science USA*, 100(10):6216–20

Chapter 4
Switching, grinding, breeding

1. Edney, A T B (1991) Nutrition and Disease, in *Canine Medicine and Therapeutics*, 3rd Edition, Eds E A Chandler, D J Thompson, J B Sutton and C J Price, Blackwell, Oxford, p 760

2. Blood, D C and Studdert, V P (1999) *Saunders Comprehensive Veterinary Dictionary*, 2nd Edition, W B Saunders, London p 708

3. Blood, D C and Studdert, V P (1999) p 950

4. Kendall, P Too much supplementation may be harmful, in *Feeding the Dog and Cat*, Uncle Ben's of Australia, Wodonga, Vic

Chapter 5
Risk management

1. NZPA (2003) Lion chokes to death in front of crowd, *Sydney Morning Herald*, March 14 Web: http://195.146.173.153/lionchokesinfreakaccident.htm

2. Buogo, C et al (1995) [Presence of Campylobacter spp., Clostridium difficile, C. perfringens and salmonellae in litters of puppies and in adult dogs in a shelter] *Schweiz Arch Tierheilkd*, 137(5):165–71

3. Gorman, R Bloomfield, S Adley, C C (2002) A study of cross-contamination of food-borne pathogens in the domestic kitchen in the Republic of Ireland, *International Journal of Food Microbiology*, 5;76 (1–2):143–50

4. Consumers Union of US, Inc (1998) Chicken: What you don't know can hurt you, *Consumer Reports Online*, March 1998 Web: www.consumerreports.org/@@uPXKTo QM1LSupw4A/Categories/FoodHealth/Reports/9803chk0.htm

5. Tjalsma, E J (1990) [3 cases of Clostridium botulinum type C intoxication in the dog], *Tijdschr Diergeneeskd*, 1;115(11):518–21

6. Washington State University (2004) Salmon Poisoning Disease, *College of Veterinary Medicine, Pet Health Topics*, Web: www.vetmed.wsu.edu/ClientED/salmon.asp

7. Salwa, A (2004) A natural outbreak of Aujeszky's disease in farm animals, *Polish Journal of Veterinary Science*, 7(4):261–6

8. Torda, A (2001) Toxoplasmosis. Are cats really the source? *Australian Family Physician*, 30(8):743–7

9. Gamble, H R and Patton, S (200) Pork Safety, *Facts*, National Pork Producers

Council, Web: www.meatscience.org/Pubs/factsheets/toxoplasma.pdf

10. Lindsay, D S Blagburn, B L, Dubey, J P (1992) Factors affecting the survival of Neospora caninum bradyzoites in murine tissues, *Journal of Parasitology*, 78(1):70–2

11. Jacobs, D E and Fox, M T (1991) Endoparasites, in *Canine Medicine and Therapeutics*, 3rd Edition, Eds E A Chandler, D J Thompson, J B Sutton, & C J Price, Blackwell Scientific Publications, Oxford, p 718

12. Soulsby, E J L (1982) Echinococcus Rudolphi, 1801, in Helminths, *Arthropods and Protozoa of Domesticated Animals*, 7th Edition, Baillière Tindall, London, pp 119–123

13. Stevenson, W J and Hughes, K L (1988) Parasitic diseases, in *Synopsis of Zoonoses in Australia*, 2nd edition, Australian Government Publishing Service, Canberra, p 173

14. BARFWorld (2005) Web: www.barfworld.com

15. University of Maryland Medical Centre (2004) Glucosamine, Web: www.umm.edu/ altmed/ConsSupplements/Glucosaminecs.html

Chapter 6
Nasty diseases

1. Carroll, L (1997) Chapter 7 A Mad Tea-Party, in *Alice's Adventures in Wonderland*, Puffin, London p 76

2. Spurlock, M (2004) *Super Size Me* Documentary film Web: www.supersizeme.com/

3. Myers, L (2003) Predilection to dental calculus formation in a group of dogs: Influence of calculus on the sense of smell, *2003 International Working Dog Breeding Conference Program*, Web: www.iwdba.org reported in *RMB Newsletter* 4:2 Web: www.rawmeatybones.com

4. Waltham Centre for Pet Nutrition advertisement (2002) *Veterinary Times*, 15 July 32:27

5. Lonsdale, T (1995) Periodontal disease and leucopenia, *Journal of Small Animal Practice*, 36, 542–546

6. Moxham, G (2001) The Waltham Feces Scoring System—a tool for veterinarians and pet owners: How does your pet rate? *Waltham Focus* 11:2 24–25

7. Burrows, C F and Ignaszewski, L A (1990) Canine gastric dilatation-volvulus, *Journal of Small Animal Practice*, 31, 495–501

8. Kronfeld, D S (1979) Common Questions About the Nutrition of Dogs and Cats, *Compendium on Continuing Education* 1:1

9. Blood, D C and Studdert, V P (1999) *Saunders Comprehensive Veterinary Dictionary*, 2nd Edition, W B Saunders, London p 832

10. Zoran, D L (2002) The carnivore connection to nutrition in cats, *Journal of the American Veterinary Medical Association*, 221:11 1559–1567

11. Grossi, S G, Genco, R J (1998) Periodontal disease and diabetes mellitus: a two-way relationship, *Annals of Periodontology*, 3 (1):51–61

12. Charles, J (1996) Polyuria/Polydipsia in *The Art and Science of Diagnosis: A practical approach*, Proceedings of 23rd ASAVA Annual Conference 1996, Bondi, p 34

13. Meurman, J H Sanz, M and Janket, S J (2004) Oral health, atherosclerosis, and cardiovascular disease, *Critical Reviews in Oral Biology & Medicine*, 1;15(6):403-13

14. Dogtor, J (2001) The Answer to "Why is the Plane of Our Nation's Health in a Death Spiral?" Web: http://dogtorj.tripod.com/id4.html

15. Mugford, R A (1987) The influence of nutrition on canine behaviour, *Journal of Small Animal Practice*, 28, 1046–1055

16. Smith, B and Devlin, P (2000) Enhancing puppy immune response through diet, *Waltham Focus* 10:4 32–31

17. Lonsdale, T (1995)

18. World Cancer Research Fund/American Institute for Cancer Research (1997) Scientific evidence and judgement, in *Food, Nutrition and the Prevention of Cancer: a global perspective*, American Institute for Cancer Research, Washington, p 72

Chapter 7
Dentistry matters

1. British Small Animal Veterinary Association (2003) Diet& Feeding, in *Scamp's Diary: The BSAVA pet care guide*, 4th Edition, British Small Animal Veterinary Association, Lifecycle Marketing Limited, Maidenhead p 32

2. Harvey, C E and Emily, P (1993) Function, Formation, and Anatomy of Oral Structures in Carnivores, in *Small Animal Dentistry*, Mosby, St Louis, p 6 (Eruption schedules vary with breed and size of animal.)

3. Cromie, W J (2002) Discovering who lives in your mouth: Bacteria give clues to cancer and gum disease, *Harvard University Gazette*, August 22, 2002 Web: www.hno.harvard.edu/gazette/2002/08.22/01-oralcancer.html

4. West-Hyde, L and Floyd, M (1994) Dentistry, in *Textbook of Veterinary Internal Medicine*, 4th Edition (Eds Ettinger S J and Feldman E C) W B Saunders, Philadelphia, p 1104

5. Margulis, L and Sagan, D (1997) Chapter 4 Entering the Microcosm, in *Microcosmos: Four billion years of microbial evolution*, University of California Press pp 69–83

6. Coghlan, A (1996) Slime City, *New Scientist*, 2045 p 34

7. Liébana, J and Castillo, A (1994) Physiopathology of primary periodontitis associated with plaque. Microbial and host factors. A review. Part 2. *Australian Dental Journal*, 39(5):310–5

8. Liébana, J and Castillo, A (1994)

9. DuPont, G A (1998) Prevention of Periodontal disease, *Veterinary Clinics of North America, Small Animal Practice*, 28(5):1129–45

10. Waltham Centre for Pet Nutrition advertisement (2002) *Veterinary Times*, 15 July 32:27

11. Lonsdale, T (2001) The Bite on Veterinary Dentistry, in *Raw Meaty Bones: Promote Health*, Rivetco P/L, NSW, Australia, p 191

12. Dental health Information, Your smile: Gums are just as important as teeth. Dental Health Foundation – Australia, The University of Sydney, S82

13. Wilson, G J (1999) Slab Fractures of Carnassial Teeth in Dogs, *Australian Veterinary Practitioner*, 29:2 84–85

14. Abbott, P V (1996) The changing face of dentistry. Endodontics, Insert in: *News Bulletin*, Australian Dental Association, April 1996 232

15. Oguntebi, B R (1994) Dentine tubule infection and endodontic therapy implications, *International Endodontic Journal*, 27(4):218–22

16. Wilson, G J (1999)

Chapter 8
Sound and vision

1. Personal communication from several professional dog trainers.

2. Phillips, K (2005) *Dog Bite Law*, Web: www.dogbitelaw.com/

3. Mugford, R A (1987) The influence of nutrition on canine behaviour, *Journal of Small Animal Practice*, 28, 1046–1055

4. Myers, L (2003) Predilection to dental calculus formation in a group of dogs: Influence of calculus on the sense of smell, *2003 International Working Dog Breeding Conference Program*, Web: www.iwdba.org reported in *RMB Newsletter* 4:2 Web: www.rawmeatybones.com

5. Parslow RA, et al, (2005) Pet ownership and health in older adults: findings from a survey of 2,551 community-based Australians aged 60-64, *Gerontology*, 51(1):40-7

6. Lonsdale, T (1995) Periodontal disease and leucopenia, *Journal of Small Animal Practice*, 36, 542–546

7. Lonsdale, T (2001) Foul-mouth AIDS, in *Raw Meaty Bones: Promote Health*, Rivetco P/L, NSW, Australia, p 148–9

8. Buffington, T (2002) Feeding Our Pets, *Public Interest*, National Public Radio, August 8 2002 Web: Radio Interviews www.rawmeatybones.com

INDEX

———◆———

A

abattoirs 38
aggression
  diet and 62, 91, 93
  epileptic seizures 73
  while feeding 36
anaesthesia for tooth removal 84
anatomy of the jaw 78–80
animals, wild 10–1, 40
antioxidants 73
appetite 27
artificial bones 77
Aujeszky's disease 56

B

bacteria 54–6
  in the mouth 80–2
'barf' 60–1
beef 22, 101
bile, vomiting 52
biofilm bacteria 81
biological problems with raw food
  51–8
biting, see aggression
bloat 69
blood lust myth 62
blood vessels, effect of junk food 71
bogus problems 62–3
bones, see also raw food
  need for in diet 77–88
  stuck in esophagus 53
botulinum toxin 55
bowel lining 66, 69

brain chemicals 13, 72–3
breath, see dog breath
breeding, nutrition for 48–9
broken teeth 85
BSE, see mad cow disease
Buffington, Tony 95
bulk food 33, 38–9
bull terriers 54
butchering at home 34
butchers 35, 37, see also human-grade
  food
buyers' cooperatives 38–9

C

calcium, for puppies 49
calculus 69, 81
Campylobacter 55
cancer 74
canine teeth 78–9, see also deciduous
  teeth
canned foods 66
carbohydrates, not required by dogs 13
carcasses
  buying for food 32
  feeding from 11–2, 101
  in diet 18–9
  proportions of bone and meat 25
carnivores, in the wild 11
cat feces, in diet 24
cellulose, not required by dogs 13
chicken, see poultry
chocolate, toxic to pets 60
choking 53

PHOTOGRAPHS

GIDGET DEVOURS A CHICKEN FRAME

Photos: Courtesy Irene Hordicek

CHICKEN FOR DINNER
CELERES NASYIIAT
AGED 16 WEEKS

RAW PORK
1 SALUKI AND
6 AZAWAKH PUPPIES
AGED 9 WEEKS

GREEN TRIPE, YUM
AZAWAKH PUPPIES
AGED 9 WEEKS

Photos: Courtesy Alison Tyler

JED 'FLOSSING' ON
A CHICKEN FRAME

TATUM 'FLOSSING' ON
A KANGAROO TAIL

TATUM AND PODGE
PICKING OVER TABLE SCRAPS

PODGE AND HANK
A HARE, MUCH TOO GOOD TO SHARE

JED AGED 6 WEEKS

JED AGED 1 YEAR
AND THE AUTHOR

ACKNOWLEDGEMENTS

Many generous people have helped to communicate the raw meaty bones message. In August 2001 Catherine O'Driscoll announced the publication of *Raw Meaty Bones: Promote Health* on her Canine Health Concern internet list. Jane Anderson's list, now renamed 'rawfeeding', the Dog Health, Dog Read and other lists soon helped spread the word. It was a fun time and I 'met' many people on the internet.

In March 2002 Kim Roberts hosted the first raw meaty bones seminars at the University of Western Australia, Extension. Now there is a long list of people I wish to thank. Swanie Simon and the organizers of the Gesunde Hunde Treff invited me to speak in Germany (three times). Tony and Carol O'Herlihy and the team at Bark Busters UK put on a multi-city UK tour. Alison Tyler, assisted by Sue Cosby, Chris Ostrowski and others organized a four city US tour. In 2003 Alison coordinated the Lifelong Learning lecture series at Emory University, Atlanta. In the UK Jenny Sanders, Sue Merrikin, Stephen King of Crosskeys Books, Sheila Harper and Erica Bennett of Scallywags Canine Education Centre, Attila Szkukalek of Happy Pets, Jackie Marriott, Debs Wickham, Debbie Hill, Christine Stansfield and Catherine O'Driscoll together with teams of helpers hosted seminars. Aysha Rowe of Addenda Publishing organized the 2003 New Zealand tour. Lauren Elgie, ever resourceful, hosted a lecture at the Guide Dog Services in Auckland. Marina Epifani coordinated two well-attended meetings in the San Francisco Bay Area in 2004.

Back home in Australia the support team of family, computer guru, Bill Bowes and office manager Irene Hordicek keep the wheels turning. Efforts to persuade vets to contemplate the enormity of their situation mostly center on the UK Royal College of Veterinary Surgeons elections. Vets Bill Miller and Roger Meacock work in the front line and Johan Joubert contributes his enthusiasm and veterinary dental expertise. For the future I place immense faith in the teams coordinating the UK and Aussie RMB Support & Action Groups. Their efforts and determination receive my utmost respect.

Work Wonders owes its existence to Alison Tyler's cajoling and the suggestions of many. The exquisite ceramic sculptures of Youlia Anderson, Furrytale Ceramic Studio, provided inspiration for the cover. I thank Bonny Bullock for the art work and all those who helped with the design and production of the book. Any weaknesses are my responsibility; the strengths derive from a team effort.

Raw Meaty Bones:
Promote Health

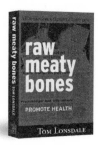

For the price of a 15 minute consultation with your vet *Raw Meaty Bones: Promote Health* provides hours of reading pleasure. In 389 easy-to-read pages you can discover masses of information not available in whole libraries of veterinary textbooks. Part history, part fascinating new science, the book reads more like a novel—but it's all peer-reviewed fact. Whether you are interested in the diet, health and welfare of pets, the stranglehold of the multi-national corporations or the dynamic potential of new scientific thinking, then *Raw Meaty Bones* is for you.

Congratulations! Your book reads superbly... I've just read it tonight, in a single sitting.
Mark O'Connor *(Poet of the Sydney, 2000 Olympic Games)*

The book is a FANTASTIC read.
Catherine O'Driscoll *(Canine Health Concern)*

Thanks for the book—BRAVO Tell the people who won't review their views that: 'The foolish and the dead never change their opinions.' Maybe that is an overstatement—as the 'brain-dead' may also refuse to revise.
Dr Tom Hungerford OBE *(Founding Director, Post Graduate Foundation in Veterinary Science, University of Sydney)*

Every graduate and undergraduate veterinarian should read the book for it has the potential to challenge the things they believe to be true, and gives them the wonderful opportunity to step back from themselves and to look more dispassionately and more deeply at the science they practise and to realise how important it is to listen carefully to others who may have a pearl of wisdom to share.
Dr Douglas Bryden AM *(Veterinary Educator and Consultant)*

Forty years ago a book called *Silent Spring* became a best seller and kick started the green movement. Its author, Rachel Carson, examined the impact of agricultural chemicals on land, waterways and living creatures including ourselves. It also examined the corporate entities that profited by developing, producing and selling the chemicals. Just a quarter of the way into Dr Tom Lonsdale's *Raw Meaty Bones: Promote Health* the thought crossed my mind that here was a *Silent Spring* for companion dogs and cats. By the time I was halfway through I was in no doubt.
Judy McMahon *The Canine Journal*

Available in bookstores and online at www.rawmeatybones.com